# BUCKINGHAM COUNTY, VIRGINIA
# SURVEYOR'S PLAT BOOK
# 1762–1858

Second Edition

TRANSCRIBED AND EDITED BY
ERIC G. GRUNDSET

CLEARFIELD

Copyright © 1983, 1996 by Eric G. Grundset
All Rights Reserved.

Second Edition
Reprinted for
Clearfield Company, Inc. by
Genealogical Publishing Co., Inc.
Baltimore, Maryland
1996, 1998, 2002

International Standard Book Number: 0-8063-4653-1

*Made in the United States of America*

ACKNOWLEDGEMENTS

Special thanks

to my wife Paula Hollis Grundset for helping transcribe and index these abstracts;

to Mrs. Ruth Johnson of Carrollton, Illinois (formerly of Fairfax, Virginia) for indexing half of the book;

to Mrs. Sharon Boone Hamner of Chapel Hill, North Carolina (formerly of Charlottesville, Virginia) and Mrs. June W. Johnson of Fairfax for offering constant encouragement in producing this volume;

and to my mother, Mrs. Evelyn Hamner Grundset of Vienna, Virginia for giving me an interest and awareness of family and history.

Dedication

The first edition of this book, published in 1983, was dedicated to our daughter Leah Amanda Grundset. Since then, our second daughter, Lara Allison Grundset was born in 1987. This 1996 revised edition is dedicated to both of our children, who have deep family roots in Buckingham County, Virginia.

PREFACE

Buckingham County was formed in 1761 from the portion of Albemarle County below the Fluvanna/James River. In 1869 The county courthouse burned, and most records were destroyed. For those whose families have lived in Buckingham, this loss has made genealogical and historical research extremely difficult. Besides family records and official records on the state level, little else remains to help the researcher.

A surprising survivor from Buckingham's old records is the Surveyor's Plat Book (1762-1858). The original volume remains in the office of the Clerk of the Circuit Court, Buckingham County. A photographic copy is in the Virginia State Archives, part of the Library of Virginia, in Richmond. Microfilm copies are available at the Library of Virginia and through the Family History Library in Salt Lake City, Utah.

This record book is a major clue to the location of numerous tracts of land in the county. When used with modern plat maps, land tax records (1782 to the present), and other post-1869 sources, the researcher should be able to piece together more information on families and farms. Every tract is not, of course, included, but many are.

Until the publication of the first edition of this book, the only index to these plats was one at the Library of Virginia listing the names of the persons for whom each survey was drawn. The abstracts and index in this publication include the names of every person and place appearing in the Surveyor's Plat Book. The plats show neighbors' land (abutters), creeks, rivers, mountains, road, and ferries. All of these have been noted and indexed. Because of the history of the division of Virginia's counties, researchers should be aware of the fact that the northeastern-most tip of original Buckingham County was added to Cumberland County in 1778 and the southern quarter of Buckingham was taken to form part of the new Appomattox County in 1845. As a result, this book of land maps includes many tracts in Appomattox as well as Buckingham and possibly a few in Cumberland.

Including copies of the actual plats was impossible. The Library of Virginia can provide copies for a fee. Reference should be made to the manuscript page numbers when requesting a copy. These are also the pages used in the index for this publication. Request prices for copying before sending an order to the library.

In the Virginia State Archives are three volumes containing surveys from Buckingham County. The abstracts in this book are from only one of these volumes. The dates in the title refer to the inclusive dates of surveys in the longer volume, 1762-1858. Most plats in this manuscript, however, pre-date 1820. A comparison with the other two volumes shows that there are many surveys in these two books not included in these published abstracts. In addition, some surveys which do appear in this publication have slightly different information recorded in the other manuscripts. A second volume of abstracts from the other two books is planned for the near future.

My interest in Buckingham County stems from the fact that many of my maternal ancestors have lived in the county since it was a part of Albemarle and possibly Goochland. Research on these families has varied in difficulty depending on the records kept by each. Correspondence regarding any of the following families is welcome: Hamner, Spencer, Patteson, Glover, Clopton, Dibrell, Morgan, Tindall, and Benning.

Every effort has been made to transcribe names and other information from the plats exactly as they appeared. In most instances the copy in the Library of Virginia is very clear. Obscured areas result from defects in the original manuscript, such as torn pages or water damage. I gratefully accept any corrections.

The map is intended to serve as a general location guide to place names and not as a detailed depiction of the Buckingham landscape. [On several occasions since 1983, this map has been reprinted in other books without permission and without credit to this author. This occured most recently in 1995, although the individual responsible has sent corrections to everyone who purchased his book.] More detailed maps are available from the U.S. Geological Survey and a current property map is in the Buckingham County Clerk's Office, Buckingham, Virginia.

Good luck with your Buckingham County research!

Eric G. Grundset
5200 Marvell Lane
Fairfax, Virginia 22032
February 1996

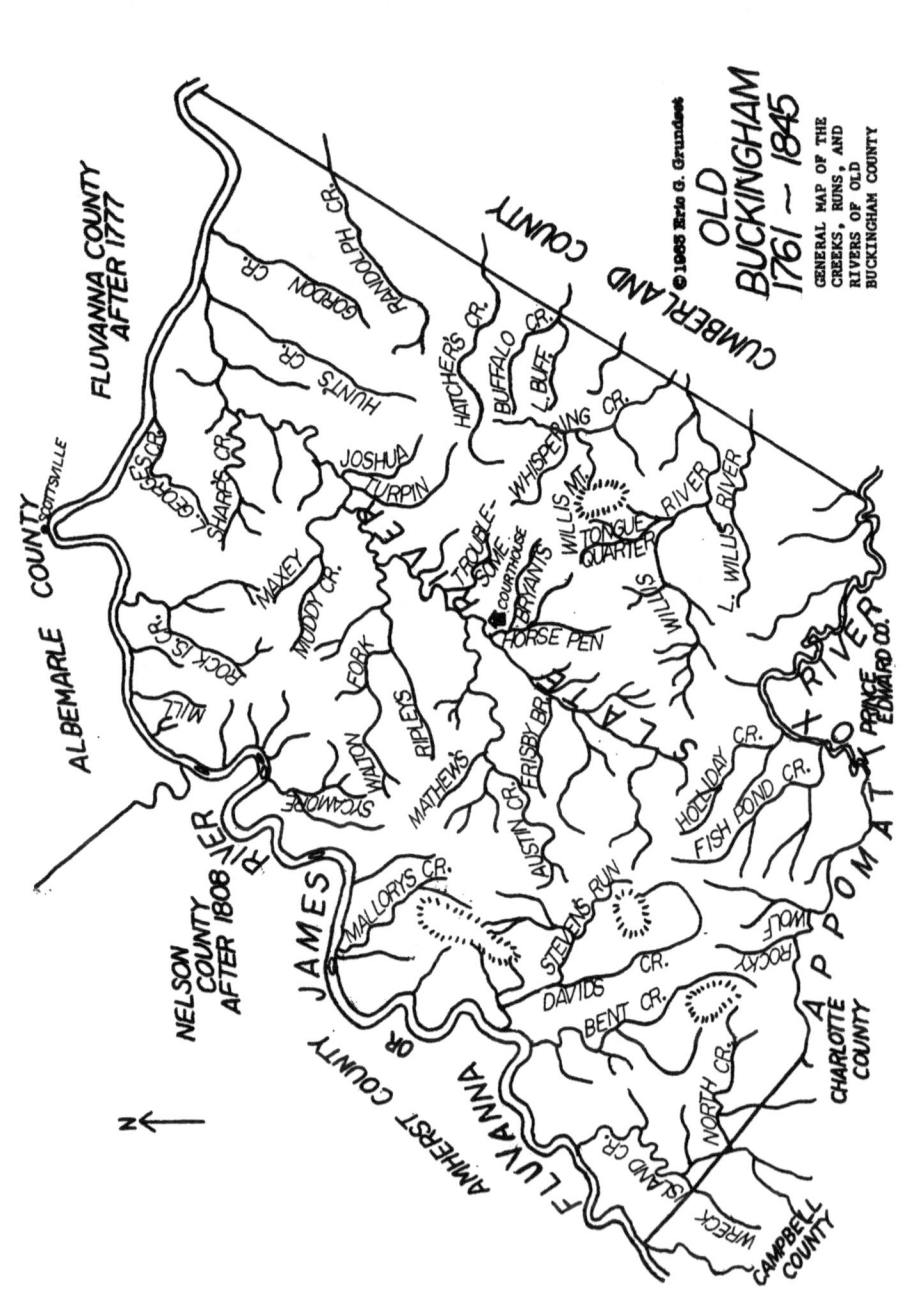

## Page 1

Hickerson Barksdale Feb. 23 1762; 275 ac.; on Cattail, Long Branch Cattail, South Fork Willis' Creek; William Curd, John Sanders, new lines, Alex Stinson neighbors.

Hickerson Barksdale; Feb. 23. 1762; 275 ac.; Cattail and others; John Sanders, Alex. Stinson (2 lines), and Barksdale's own lines.

William Gregory; Dec. 1, 1762; 64 ac.; north side Appomattox; John Peck Jr., John Woodall, William Gregory's own lines; John Wright neighbors.

Edmund Wood; Dec. 2, 1762; 200 ac.; north side Appomattox; Wood's own lines, Nath. Hoggart neighbors.

## Page 2

John Ridgway; April 27, 1763; 142 ac.; both sides Doe Creek; Col. Fry, Benjamin Arnold, James Grey neighbors; transferred to Littleberry Epperson of Buckingham

Henry Baird; Dec. 14, 1762; 67 ac.; west side Willis' mountain; Joseph Childress, David Maloy neighbors.

Benjamin Arnold; April 26, 1763; 285 ac.; heads of branches of Willis' Creek and Buck & Doe; Stephen Sanders, John Snody, George Hooper, Joshua Fry dec'd, new lines, neighbors.

George Chambers; Dec. 15, 1763 (?) mutilated; 90 ac.; part of Willis' Mountain called W--- Rocky Ridge; Col. Bolling, Chamber's own lines, new lines, neighbors.

## Page 3

William Johnson; Feb. 16, 1763; 300 ac.; head branches Childress' Creek; William Weeklin, Stephen Chenault, Col. Fry, John Hughes, new lines neighbors; transferred to William Garland and included with Joseph Epperson's plat of 186 ac.

John Childres; Oct. 15, 1763; foot of Willis Mountain called Round Top; W. John Nicholas, his own.lines, Willis Mountain neighbors; 40 ac.

Joseph Epperson; Feb. 16, 1763; head branch Tongue Quarter Creek and a head of Childres' Creek; 186 ac.; William Weeklin, John Vest, Willis' Mountain, ---- Hays.

John Vest; April 26, 1763; 60 ac.; on a ridge among branches of Willis' Creek; John Nicholas, Thomas Jefferson neighbors

## Page 4

Joseph Colland; Feb. 15, 1763; 307 ac.; ridges on heads of branches of Slate River and Troublesome Creek; John Glover, G. Thomas, Mathew Agee,

Samuel Glover, Brian Dolan, Hugh Cass neighbors.

Nathan Northcut; March 29, 1764; 262 ac.; head branches of George's Creek of Rock Island; William Anglin and Pet. Bondurant neighbors.

Thomas Truman Murphey; November 18, 1764; 400 ac.; branches South Fork Slate River; new lines, Murphey's own lines, John Hoss (?), Thomas -----(?), John Hunter (?) neighbors.

William Phelps; Feb. 2, 1764(?); 120 ac.; south branch of the Bent ---; -----Clarke, William Diuguid, William Phelps neighbors.

## Page 5

Jeremiah Garland; March 20, 1764; 830 ac.; head branches of Briants Creek and Troublesome Creek on Glover's Road (drawn in on plat), Courthouse Road (drawn in on plat), and Hunter's Road (drawn in on plat); John and Eliza. Hay's, John Hughes, Col. F. Bakes, Issac Salley, Thompson, Hunter, John Hunter, Thos. Neuman, Thos. Truman Murphey neighbors.

Griffin Garland; November 18, 1764; 1000 ac.; branch of Slate River and head branch of Woodson Creek; John Hunter, new lines, Shachevel Whitebread; Thos. Truman Murphy neighbors.

William Phelps; February 22, 1764; 92 ac.; on west side of David's Creek; Thos. Thornill, Phelps' own line, Francis Wagstaff neighbors.

## Page 6

Harden Purkins; November 23, 1763; 400 ac.; branch of Rock Island and branch of George's Creek on south side Fluvanna River; his own lines; no neighbors indicated.

Thomas Thornill; February 22, 1764; 250 ac.; both sides Stephens Creek and joining David's Creek (creeks drawn in); no neighbors indicated.

Robert Spooner Bailey; March 29, 1764; 263 ac.; south branch Rock Island Creek; no neighbors indicated; certificate granted William Amg--- February 12, 1783 because Bailey did not pay surveyor's fee.

## Page 7

William Gilliam; February 7, 1764; 240 ac.; among south branches of Wreck Island Creek; John Gannaway, John Cox, James Phelps neighbors.

William Gilliam; February 7, 1764; 187 ac.; south side Wreck Island Creek; John Coleman, John Cox's new lines, neighbors.

Robert Ransone; 328 ac.; August 17, 1764; north branch Appomattox River; no neighbors indicated.

Edward Maxey; March 24, 1764; 400 ac.; north side Slate River and joining same below mouth of Great Creek (river shown); William Baber, ----Maxey, Ric'd Gwin, new line, Hugh Moore's line.

## Page 8

Mark Doss; February 14, 1764; among branches of South side Wreck Island Creek; his own lines, James Phelps neighbor.

John Cox; February 9, 1764; 282 ac.; on both sides Wreck Island Creek; John Coleman, Jeremiah Whitney neighbors.

John Cox; February 13, 1764; 99 ac.; north side Coleman's Run of Wreck Island Creek; John Coleman (on two sides).

Peter Guerrant; March 26, 1764; 225 ac.; among branches south side Hunts; Capt. William Allen, Peter Guerrants own lines neighbors.

## Page 9

Charles Parrow; March 26, 1764; 248 ac.; both sides large branch on the south side Hunt Creek; his own lines; no neighbors indicated.

Briant Doland; February 25, 1764; 219 ac.; branches of Phriebys Creek; Nicholas Connors, new lines, John Lee neighbors.

James Meredith; Feburary 25, 1764; 243 ac.; branches David's Creek; new lines; his own lines, Thomas Thornill neighbor.

John Flower; February 24, 1764; 39 ac.; both sides Mimm's Creek; William Kelley, Abra. Smith neighbors.

## Page 10

Charles Layne; February 14, 1764; 270 ac.; south branches Wreck Island Creek; James Phelps, William Megginson, William Gilliam, Mark Doss neighbors.

James Meredith; February 25, 1764; 50 ac.; side of Slate River Mountain; no neighbors indicated.

William Baber; March 24, 1764; 400 ac.; both sides great creek of Slate River and Freeland's Lick Branch; his own land, Sampson Maxey, Isaiah Burton neighbors.

Richard Murray; March 28, 1764; 380 ac.; on branches George's Creek on south side Fluvanna River; Col. Jefferson dec'd neighbor.

Joseph Epperson; December 16, 1763; 178 ac.; south branches Bollings Creek; Stephen Chenalt; his own lines, William Weeklin, John Vest, Francis Childress, Mr. John Nicholas neighbors.

## Page 11

John May Sr.; September 13, 1764; 400 ac.; ridges and heads of branches of Elk Creek; James Phelps, new lines, William Diuguid, William Megginson,

Charles Layne, new lines neighbors.

John May Sr.; September 13, 1764; 260 ac.; ridge between Diuguid's Mill Creek and Elk Creek; William Diuguid dec'd neighbor.

Joshua May; February 11, 1764; 170 ac.; ridges and heads of branches of Diuguid's Mill Creek; William Diuguid dec'd, Colo Turpin, James Phelps.

## Page 12

Richard Epperson; September 28, 1764; 400 ac.; head branches Willis' Creek and Slate River; new lines on two sides, Richard Epperson's own land, John Hunter, Patrick O'Brian neighbors.

Joseph Epperson; September 28, 1764; 744 ac.; heads of branches of Buck & Doe Creek; new lines, Richard Epperson, William Akers, James Gray, John Ridgeway and his father's lines, Shac Whitebread, new lines, neighbors.

George Wright; October 24, 1764; 286 ac.; both sides Appomattox in Buckingham and Prince Edward Counties; 225 in Buckingham and 61 in Prince Edward; joined by Virtue of order of Council for George Wright; William Gregory and Nath. Haggatt neighbors.

## Page 13

John Cabell; October 11, 1764; among branches on south side Fluvanna River; Eliz.(?) Birk, own lines; 400 ac.

John Cabell; October 12, 1764; 90 ac.; south side Fluvanna River; no neighbors indicated.

John Jennings; September 25, 1764; 30 ac.; north side Appomattox River; Edm'd Wood dec'd, Charles May, own lines, neighbors.

## Page 14

Henry Pruitt; October 10, 1764; 150 ac.; south Branches David's Creek; no neighbors indicated.

Joseph Evans; March 22, 1765; 80 ac.; both sides south branch of David's Creek; no neighbors indicated.

Richard Murray; April 12, 1765; 183 ac; north side little George's Creek in Buchingham; Richard Murray, Thomas Ballowe neighbors.

George Wilson; March 22, 1765; 82 ac.; south side Fluvanna River and joining the same; no neighbors indicated.

## Page 15

James Freeland; March 21, 1765; 64 ac.; south side Fluvanna River and joining river; no neighbors indicated.

Mathew Landers; April 16, 1765; 59 ac.; on and among small branches on north side Rock Island Creek; Moses Ray, John Bailey neighbors.

David Low; April 15, 1765; 174 ac.; on both sides Rock Island Creek; Ben. Howard, Col. James Jordan, Rob. S. Bailey neighbors.

Josias Jones; March 24, 1765; 425 ac.; both sides Philip's Creek; James Meridith, Alexander Smith, own lines.

## Page 16

David McCormick; March 17, 1767; 282 ac.; on head branch of Willis' River; Epaphroditus Guilliam, Lambeth T. Blackbourn, new lines, own lines.

Nath. Finch; March 18, 1767; 90 ac.; head branches Willis River; The Great Road, new lines, David McCormick, new lines.

Anderson Adcock; March 26, 1768; 38 ac.; ridges between waters Bolling and Whispering Creeks on both branches of Willis's River; Robert Bolling, Robert Moore, James Rudd, new lines.

Thomas Lee; March 19, 1767; 176½ ac.; both sides Fish Pond Creek; ---- Hall, ---- Roberts, vacant land, other illegible; note at bottom partly illegible; carries a date of August 12, 1801; John Patteson mentioned.

## Page 17

Jeremiah Whitney Gent., Richard Taylor, Thomas Mathews; June 22, 1768; 379 ac.; ridges and heads of branches between Fluvanna River and Wreck Island Creek; James Christian, new lines, William Phelps, new lines, W. C. Whitney neighbors; Coleman's Road shown dividing survey; division within survey to William Phelps (mulatto) by order Governor and Council and a certificate granted to ?? Gent.

Thomas Stevens; June 24, 1768; 73 ac.; fork of David's Creek; William Megginson neighbor; new road shown.

Charles Patteson (O.R.); February 22, 1769; 341 ac.; both sides Mims' Creek and on spur of Slate River Mountain and bounded by adjacent plot; creek and Megginson's Road shown; Col. James Cabell's Road shown; Thos. Matthew's Road shown; Col. Cabell and new lines.

## Page 18

William Anglin; February 21, 1769; 333 ac.; on ridges between Slate River and Turpin's Creek; John Bondurant, new line, Thos. Turpin (on two sides), new lines, Benj. Goss, Nehemiah Mackishan neighbors.

Thomas Matthews; February 23, 1769; 340 ac.; branches David's Creek; new lines; T. Matthews own land, Francis Wagstaff neighbors.

Jeremiah Whitney Gent., Richard Taylor, Thomas Matthews; February 20, 1769; 392 ac.; on Fluvanna River and joining lines of James Christian.

## Page 19

Jeremiah Whitney Gent.; February 28, 1769; 46 ac.; on ridges and branches between Fluvannah (sic) River and Wreck Island Creek; new lines, James Christian, Whitney-Taylor-Matthews new lines, neighbors.

William Gilliam; November 25, 1769; 46 ac.; branch of Holiday River and ridges adjacent to his own lines.

Lambeth Tye Blackbourn; November 25, 1769; south branches of Willis' River and ridges adjacent to his own lands and Epaphroditus Guilliam.

Thomas Goodsey; November 28, 1769; 67 ac.; on Sam's Creek a branch of Slate River; new lines, Thomas Goodsey, Allen Tye neighbors; transferred to Thomas Newcome of Cumberland County May 16, 1777; transferred by Newcome to William Hensley March 11, 1780; transferred by William Hensley to Nathaniel Garratt March 7, 1781.

Nathl Garratt; November 28, 1769; 127 ac.; main ridges between Willis' and Slate River the draughs of the water courses on each side the ridge are Buck & Doe and Sam's Creek; ----Epperson, Will Hensley, one illegible neighbors.

## Page 20

William Warren ; December 2, 1769; 79 ac.; south side Willis River joining earlier survey; new lines, ----Easley neighbor.

William Low; December 29, 1769; 36 ac.; branches Willis' River; Robert Sanders and his own land neighbors.

David W. McCormick; December 24, 1770; 390 ac.; north side Holladay River joining Beard's Road and lines of William W. McCormick; by an attested order transferred to Benj. Hodges who the same day transferred the land to Hickerson Barkesdale.

W. Wilkinson; May 22, 1771; 30 ac.; south side Philip's Creek joining Colo. George Carrington, Walter King (now of Great Britain) and W. Wilkinson.

William Phelps (mulatto); August 21, 1771; 378 ac.; branches Wreck Island Creek and joining Jeremiah Whitney Gent.; new lines, ----Christian neighbor

## Page 21

George Hooper (Gent.); December 12, 1771; 200 ac.; north draughs of Willis' River between lines of Fry, Nicholas, Epperson, Jefferson and George Hooper (Gent.); neighbors: George Hooper's own land, John Nicholas, new lines, Colo John Fry, Nath. Epperson.

Theodorick Webb; July 20, 1775; 200 ac.; lower fork Thomas' Creek and joining lines of John Counch, Benjamin Howard dec'd, George Damson, and John

Bowcock; transferred to John Couch.

William Flowers; March 21, 1775; 120 ac.; head north fork of David's Creek. Charles Patteson (O.R.) and Thomas Blakey neighbors; surveyed by David Walker, assistant surveyor; transferred to Charles Patteson (O.R.)

Henry Bell; November 1, 1775; 28 ac.; on south branches of Hatcher's Creek called Mill Quarter Branch; Reane Chastain, Patrick O' Brian, Bell's own land neighbors.

Thomas Boaz; March 15, 1771; 72 ac.; north fork Holladay River; joining his own land; transferred to Joseph Payne.

Thomas Boaz; March 19, 1771; 158 ac.; north fork Holladay River and on both sides of road known as Buckingham or Baird's Road; no neighbors indicated.

### Page 22

Thomas Matthews; March 19, 1771; 128 ac.; on head branches of dry Beaver Pond Creek; Richard Taylor and new lines neighbors.

James Matthews; March 19, 1771; 110 ac.; head of David's Creek; William Still and new lines neighbors.

William Thornhill; March 26, 1771; 186 ac.; branches of Bent Creek and joining William Diuguid and Thornhill's own land; Works of this land is this day renewed and granted to Jno. Miller who had entered the same by warrant on 17th March 1792 (dated November 20, 1793).

Ralph Flowers; November 12, 1772; 150 ac.; both sides Middle River of Slate River and joining old lands of Ralph Flowers.

Francis Amos; November 12, 1772; 518 ac.; branches of Middle Fork of Slate River joining Nicholas Conner and new lines.

### Page 23

John Brown; November 16, 1772; 70 ac.; branches of David's Creek on west side of Naked Mountain joining William Patteson and John Brown's own land and new lines.

John Patteson (word "Jr" crossed out after his name); November 17, 1772; 170 ac.; east branches of David's Creek joining Nicholas Maynaird, Thomas Matthews and John Patteson and new lines.

John Booker Hay; January 30, 1773; 72 ac.; head branches of Appomattox River between lines of John Patteson, James Fox, David Tyrie, and Thomas Phelps.

William Patteson; November 18, 1772; 224 ac.; branches David's Creek and joining Church Road, Nicholas Maynaird, William Clark, James Burnett, William Patteson's own land and new lines.

David Patteson; March 11, 1773; 165 ac.; both sides Cycamore (sic) Island Creek and joining David Patteson (A.B.).

## Page 24

James Burnett; November 19, 1772; 157 ac.; west branches David's Creek and joining William Clark and James Burnett's own land.

John Patteson, Jr.; November 19, 1772; 347 ac.; west branches David's Creek joining William Clark, Thomas Still (Hill?), ----Mayo, John Brown and John Patteson Jrs own land.

Thomas Doss; November 30, 1772; 92 ac.; branches Wreck Island Creek; joining William Diuguid, William Gilliam, Thomas Doss' own land, Charles Witt, and new lines.

Robert Wright; December 1, 1772; 196 ac.; on branches Wreck Island Creek joining Thomas Doss, Alexander Smith and new lines; transferred to Peter Day January 15, 1780.

James Southern; December 19, 1773; 225; on Willis's Creek and joining William Hensley.

## Page 25

John Fields; December 1, 1772; 134 ac.; branches Wreck Island Creek joining Thomas Doss, James Beckham and new lines.

Colo. Jos. Cabell; March 10, 1773; 100 ac.; south side and joining Fluvanna River and Cabell's own land and new lines.

Anthony Dubral; March 13, 1773; 415 ac.; branches Walton's Fork and branches of Slate River and joining Miles Gibson and Dubral's own land and new lines.

Nicholas Conner; March 1773; 504 ac.; on Walton's Fork of Slate River joining his own land and new lines.

Thomas Patteson; March 24, 1773; 296 ac.; on both sides of Nothing Branch of Wreck Island Creek also a branch of Fluvanna River joining James Hundley, Benjamin Witt and Patteson's own land and new lines.

## Page 26

Edward Ferguson; March 25, 1773; 329 ac.; both sides west fork of Woolf Creek a branch of Appomattox River and joining William Ferguson, Ezekiel Carson, Bartholemew Zachery, and Nicholas Hays; transferred to Charles Patteson (gent.) by an attested order October 14, 1776.

Thomas Smith; May 3, 1774; 380 ac.; both sides Little Fish Pond Creek a branch of Appomattox River and joining Evan Lee, Thomas Smith and new lines; transferred to James McDowell and from McDowell to William Maxey of this county April 16, 1786.

James Boyd; November 24, 1779; 156 ac.; both sides Middle River of Slate River joining Thomas Head dec'd, and now in Rich'd Williams, and new lines.

John Hardiman; November 17, 1779; 619 ac.; south branch Middle Slate
River joining Ralph Flowers and Hardiman's own lands and new lines.

## Page 27

Ralph Flowers; November 16, 1779; 382 ac.; both sides Pick Shin Road and
on south branches Middle Slate River and joining Capt. John Moseley,
Thomas Jones, and Flower's own land.

Richard Taylor; November 18, 1779; 203 ac.; south branches Middle Slate
River and joining Andrew Flowers, Nicholas Conner, Francis Amos and
new lines.

Bryant Dolling; November 19, 1779; 188 ac.; near head of Frisby's Creek
and joining John Wright, Nicholas Conner, Bryant Dolling and new lines.

Joshua Taylor; November 22, 1779; 351 ac.; both sides Slate River; no neighbors.

## Page 28

William Bryant; March 25, 1780; 126 ac.; both sides Middle River of Slate
River; joining Bryant Dolling, Nicholas Connor, Thomas Head dec'd and
new lines.

Thomas Wright; November 25, 1779; 232 ac.; location?; joining John Wright
and new lines; resurveyed November 19, 1802 for Colo John Cabell and
Hugh McCormick.

Francis Amos; date mutilated; 241 ac.; Middle Slate River joining John
Wright and Francis Amos.

Lewis Christian; date mutilated; 40 ac;. location missing; joining Anderson
Adcock, Charles Wheeler, Honorable A. Carey Esq., and W. Coseley.

## Page 29

Thomas Stevens; March 3, 1780; 114 ac.; north branches David's Creek;
joining Col. John Harris, John Stevens, Thomas Stevens; transferred
to George Coatsby by order April 5, 1781.

John Byron Goatherd; March 23, 1780; 343½ ac.; branches of David's Creek;
William Goings, Thomas Wright, and new lines neighbors.

William Patterson(Taylor)(?); March 25, 1780; 215 ac.; both sides Beaver
Pond Creek including the head; James Matthews and new lines neighbors.

Thomas Matthews; April 15, 1780; 10 ac.; south side Fluvanna River and
joining Whitney, Taylor and Matthews, John Coleman, and Mr. Christian.

Thomas Oglesby; April 17, 1780; 356½ ac.; branches of Wreck Island Creek;
Jeremiah Whitney gent., Issac Staples, and land of ----Philip's Mine
Survey neighbors.

## Page 30

Richard Taylor; April 19, 1780; 180 ac.; south branches of Fluvanna River; joining Thomas Oglesby, Philip's Mine Survey, Turner Christian, Issac Staples and new lines.

Thomas Thornhill; April 20, 1780; 404 ac.; south branches Fluvanna River; joining George Hilton, old boundary of Doctor William Cabell's River Survey and new lines.

John Stevens and Thomas Stevens; April 21, 1780; 278 and 62 ac. respectively; north branch of David's Creek; joining John Stevens (son of Thomas) Thomas (father of the said John) and new lines.

William Still; April 29, 1780; 364 ac.; near Piney Mountain on branches of Bent Creek; joining Thomas Still, William Still and new lines.

## Page 31

Thomas Matthews; April 27, 1780; 1626 ac.; both sides dry Beaver Pond Creek and branches and joining Colo. John Harris, Thomas Stevens, John Chambers, ----Waggstaff, Henry Morris and new lines.

Thomas Still; May 1, 1780; 628 ac.; branches of Bent Creek; William Still, Benjamin Patteson, Thomas Still and new lines.

## Page 32

Leonard Ballowe; March 22, 1783; 200 ac.; on Spencer's Creek a branch of Walton's Fork; joining William Kenneday, Anthony Dibrell and new lines.

David Patteson; March 22, 1783; 38 ac.; location ?; joining Anthony Dibrell, Little B. Mosby, and Mr. McDonald.

James Smith; April 23, 1783; 239 ac.; on Lick Creek a Branch of Slate River; Josias Jones, Elizabeth Smith and new lines.

Elizabeth Smith; April 28, 1783; 65 ac.; on ? a branch of Slate River; joining Josias Jones, Samuel Arrington, Elizabeth Smith and new lines.

## Page 33

Charles Maxey; April 4, 1783; 661 ac.; location ?; joining William Kennadey, Colo. Joseph Cabell, John Terry, Leonard Ballowe, and new lines.

John Terry; April 5, 1783; 200 ac.; branches Long and Hungry Creek; joining Dibraill, David Patteson, Colo. Joseph Cabell, Charles Maxey and Leonard Ballowe; transferred to John Patteson Jr., February 3, 1785.

David Patteson; April 5, 1783; 100 ac.; north branches Walton's fork of Slate River; joining Anthony Dibrell, Thomas Blakey and John Terry.

Thomas Patteson; April 10, 1783; 212 ac.; west side Taylor's Creek; Richard Taylor, John Terry, Colo. Joseph Cabell adjoining.

## Page 34

Samuel Hudson; April 12, 1783; 400 ac.; on main Reyon's Creek; joining new lines and David Patteson.

Nicholas Austin; April 29, 1783; 366 ac.; on Court House Road; joining Josias Jones, Thomas Sanders, Mr. Dolling and Nicholas Austin.

Charles Beazeley; date?; 400 ac.; both sides west Oak Branch of Rock Island Creek; joining William Leak's, Joseph Thomas and new lines.

## Page 35

John McMannaway; May 16, 1783; 62 ac.; west side Wreck Island Creek; joining William Gilliam, Richard Oglesby, John Booth and James Beekham.

Charles Maxey; May 1, 1783; 400 ac.; on Little Philipses Creek; joining Josias Jones and James Smith.

Archelus Austin; April 29, 1783; 200 ac.; on big Philipses Creek; joining Josias Jones and new lines.

Capt. William Perkins; May 8, 1783; 142 ac.; location?; joining James Smith, Josias Jones, said Perkins and new lines.

## Page 36

John Terry; April 10, 1783; 215 ac.; location?; joining Anthony Dibrell, Little B. Mosby, Ellex$^{er}$ (?) Smith.

Thomas Wood; April 24, 1783; 117 ac.; on small mountain near Appomattox River; joining John Beazely, dec'd, John Bostick and Thos. Wood.

William Rakes; May 26, 1783; 360 ac.; on main Walton's Fork; joining John Terry Smith, William Goff and L. Barry Mosby.

Mollary Johns; October 20, 1783; 220 ac.; both sides Ireland Creek; joining new lines.

## Page 37

John Routen; November 15, 1783; 341 ac.; both sides Main County Road; joining Tho. Gregory, John Childers, John Bostick, Tho. Blackburn, and Roulen's own lines.

John Routen; November 16, 1783; 19 ac.; north side Appomattox River; joining William Ford and David Walke.

Capt. John Couch; December 6, 1783; 411 ac.; west branches Rock Island Creek; joining Jesse Thomas, Daniel Pucket and Couch's own lines.

Page 38

Thos. Matthews; April 17, 1780; 137 ac.; head of Boring Branch; joining James Christian and Jeremiah Whitney.

Jeremiah Whitney; April 17, 1780; 100 ac.; branches Boring Branch; joining Tho. Matthews, ----Oglesby, Whitney's own lines; transferred to John Miller November 20, 1793.

Nortley Gordan; April 20, 1780; Branches Bear Branch; 167 ac.; joining James Christian and Gordan's own lines.

Nortley Gordan; April 20, 1780; 60 ac.; on Bear Branch and branches White Oak Branch; joining John Brothers and Gordan's own lines; transferred to John Miller November 20, 1793; transferred to Edw. L. Page and Thomas ---- December 1808.

Samuel Coleman; April 20, 1780; 25 ac.; on Bear Creek; joining Gordan and Coleman's own lines; transferred to him by Nortley Gordan.

Page 39

Jeremiah Whitney; April 19, 1780; 136 ac.; on Little Wreck Island Creek; joining Whitney's own lines and Thomas Oglesby.

John Wright; April 21, 1780; 322 ac.; south side Bent Creek; joining Pendleton, Christian, Nortley Gordon and Wright's own lines; transferred from Meves Arrington to John Wright.

David Kyle; April 27, 1780; 190 ac.; on David's Creek; joining Robert Freeland, John B. Gothard and Robert Kyle; transferred from Thomas Stephens to David Kyle.

John Brothers; May 2, 1780; 102 ac.; on drafts of White Oak Branch; joining Thomas Ellyson, Andrew Flowers, Ann Gordan and Brothers' own lines.

Page 40

Jesse Strange; April 27, 1780; 713 ac. in two surveys; branches Fluvanna River and David's and Bent Creeks; joining Robert Freeland, David Kyle, John B. Strange; transferred from Thomas Stevens in person to Strange; transferred to Thomas Wright August 12, 1780.

John Worley; May 3, 1780; 183 ac.; on branches Wreck Island Creek; joining David Rogers, John Worley; transferred to John Worley by Nortley Gordan; transferred to John Miller November 20, 1793.

Thomas Ellyson; May 1, 1780; 457 ac.; on Wreck Island Creek; joining Elisha Pore, James Lyle, John Burks, Mr. Christian and Andrew Flowers; transferred from Nortley Gordan.

Page 41

Alexander Smith; May 10, 1780; 487 ac.; branches Wreck Island Creek and on

Coleman's Road; joining John Worley, Issac Chernetter, Thomas Doss, Peter Day, James Lyle and Smith's own land.

Thomas Anderson; February 21, 1782; both sides Holman's Creek; 625 ac.

Daniel Puckett; November 12, 1782; 304 ac.; branches Rock Island Creek; joining John Thomas and Puckett's own land.

Page 42

James Couch; November 13, 1782; 421 ac.; branches Fluvanna and Rock Island Creek; joining John Thomas, Daniel Puckett, Beverley Low and Couch's own lands.

William Cabell Ballowe; November 14, 1782; 308 ac.; south and middle forks Hallman's Creek; joining Thomas Anderson and new lines.

William Chambers; December 10, 1782; 125 ac.; branches Arthur's Creek a branch of Slate River; joining William Handsford, Josiah Chambers, Ruben Winfree and Leonard Patteson.

Michael Damron; December 13, 1782; 132 ac.; south fork Holman's Creek and on Howard's Road; joining William C. Ballowe and Damron's own lands.

Page 43

Robert Huddlestone; April 4, 1783; 52 ac.; head of Double Trap Creek a branch of Willis' River and on Bollings Road; joining Henry Adcock, dec'd, Robert Moore and Huddlestone's own land.

Charles Cattrell; April 16, 1783; 610 ac.; Little George's Creek and Howard's and Marr's Road; joining Anthony Murray and Cattrell's own lands.

William Baber; April 16, 1783; 405 ac.; on branches Sharp's Creek; joining Peter Fore, Anthony Murray, Robert Cary and Babers own lands.

Capt. Harden Perkins; April 18, 1783; 266 ac.; on Great George's Creek; joining Randolph Jefferson, William Anglin and Perkin's own lands.

Page 44

John Jones; May 13, 1783; 1003 ac.; Lick Creek and branches Glover's Creek with other small branches of Slate River, Johns' Courthouse Road and Jones' Road; joining John Pittman, Thomas Harvey, John Duncan, John Cox, Robert Glover and Jones' own lands.

Derby Bondurant; December 11, 1783; 290 ac.; south branches Sharp's Creek; joining Joseph Goode and Bondurant's own lands.

Francis Amos; May 2, 1780; 299 ac.; main ridge on both sides Baird's Road and on heads of branches of Bent Creek and a small branch Appomattox River; joining Joseph Palmore, David Davidson, John Ferguson, Mr. Cason, William Walker and Thomas Wingfield.

## Page 45

Edward Patteson; May 3, 1780; 186 ac.; head of Fish Pond Creek; joining Thomas Still and new lines.

Capt. John Moseley; May 4, 1780; 405 ac.; branches Slate River and Sam's Creek and on Moseley's Road; joining Charles Moseley, William Hensley, Allen Tye and new lines.

Thomas Matthews; May 9, 1780; 607 ac.; on both sides Slate River Mountain and on head branches Slate River and dry Beaver Pond Creek; joining new lines; transferred to David Bell September 1788.

Connerly Mullins; ----1780; 268 ac.; on branches Slate River; joining Joshua Tayler, Richard Tayler and new lines.

## Page 46

James McNeill; September 28, 1781; 917 ac.; on Frisby's Creek; joining Colo. Joseph Cabell, Archealus Austin, James Dorum, Nicholas Conner, William Spencer, Robert Smith and Charles Maxey.

Charles Staton; March 15, 1784; 472 ac.; on south side Rock Island Creek; joining James Hill; Samuel Hudson, John Beasely, and Staton's own land.

Charles Staton; March 16, 1784; 800 ac.; west side Rock Island Creek; joining Peter Davie, Daniel Pucket, Capt. John Couch, and Staton's own lines.

## Page 47

David Pryor; March 16, 1784; 300 ac.; west side Rock Island Creek; joining Mr. John Staton.

Thomas Anderson; March 19, 1784; 800 ac.; west side Rock Island Creek; joining Micael Damron, William Cabell Ballowe, David Pryor and John Beazley.

James Staton; March 20, 1784; 700 ac.; on each side Ballowe's Creek; joining Mr. Jordan, John Bagby and Michael Damron.

## Page 48

James Ford; April 14, 1784; 72 ac.; both sides Joseph's Creek mostly on the west side; joining Isaac Sallee, Nehemiah Markenshain, William Allen and Thomas Turpin.

George Tapscott; April 26, 1784; 510 ac.; each side Howard's Road; joining Peter Bondurant, Thomas Moss (mulatto) James Couch and Charles Cotheel.

George Rice; 228 ac.; April 27, 1784; north side Howard's Road and on some head branches of Rock Island Creek; joining Isaac Sallee, Thomas Asher, James Hundly Dobbins, and own land.

Page 49

Benjamin Cotteral; February 19, 1785; 400 ac.; adjacent to Little Berry Mosby, Capt. William Perkins, and Colo. Joseph Cabell.

Charles Jones; February 20, 1785; 160 ac.; on some head branches Ripley's Creek; joining Little Berry Mosby, Capt. William Perkins and Colo. Joseph Cabell.

Capt. William Perkins; February 20, 1785; 92 ac.; joining lines of Colo. Joseph Cabell and Capt. William Perkins.

Page 50

Jesse Strange; February 24, 1785; 216 ac.; on some of west branches of Bent Creek; joining ---- Hilton, Thomas Thornhill, Mr. Kennon.

Thomas Staples; ? 25, 1785; 126 ac.; east side Bent Creek; joining John Bryan-Gothard, Thomas Wright, John Horseley, Mase Freeland and William Goins.

Henry Woldridge; date ? ; 375 ac.; head branches of Buck Creek; rest mutilated; parts of names visible; John Epperson appears in a note dated 1796.

Page 51

George Carter; date ? ; 217 ac.; branches of Buck and Doe; joining Thomas Woldridge, Mr. Fry and Mr. Jos. Curd and new lines.

Nath'l Burton; January 26, 1786; 321 ac.; adjacent to Edward Maxey, Widow Norcutt, Nath'l Maxey and Edward Maxey.

John Sanderson; January 26, 1786; 76 ac.; joining Nath'l Maxey, Mr. Halls, and ----Smith.

Page 52

Joel Drake; January 27, 1786; 245 ac.; joining Isaac Sallee, Nath'l Burton and Drake's own land.

Henry Flood; January 28, 1786; 194 ac.; joining Isaac Garrett, Johnson, William Fuqua, and Charles Garrett.

Judith Godsey; February 7, 1786; 275 ac.; joining Capt. John Moseley, William Hensley, Mr. Hancock, John Hooper, Mr. Pitman, and Patrick Smith.

Page 53

George Webb Esq.; March 9, 1786; 4555 ac.; on Randolph's, Power's and Phelp's Creek, branches of Willis' River and James River and on Glover's Road and ---- Road; escheated by the Commonwealth from Walter King (of Great Britain) and granted to George Webb, Esq., Jno. Bernard,

John Scruggs, W. Wilkerson, Arch'd Cary, Esq., Mr. Power, Isaac
Berriman, Mr. Harry; joining Bartlett Davis (280 ac.) Daniel
Taylor, Mr. Snoddy, Zacharia Talley (240 ac.).

## Page 54

Thomas Sanders; May 1, 1786; 215 ac.; joining John Cabell and his own lands.

Capt. Davis Parish; May 3, 1786; 170 ac.; both side Holloway River; joining John Walker orphan, Capt. Silas Watkins, William Peak, David Walker and new lines.

Silas Watkins; May 4, 1786; 271 ac.; adjacent to his own lines and new lines.

## Page 55

Capt. Jacob Woodson; May 5, 1786; 390 ac.; joining Rich'd Holland, James Coleman, Mr. Chiles, Flamstead Ransons.

Masenello Womack; May 6, 1786; 32 ac.; joining Mr. Holland and Womack's new lines.

Charles Perrow; May 15, 1786; 364 ac.; on Slate River; joining Colo. Samuel Jordan, Perrow's own lines and John Nicholas.

William Spencer; August 12, 1786; 400 ac.; joining Joseph Scott, Nicholas Conner, James McNeill, Robert Smith, Benjamin More, Ralph Flowers, and Spencer's own lines.

## Page 56

David Pryor; October 12, 1786; 550 ac.; on Walton's fork bounded by Colo. Joseph Cabell's road and William Goff.

James Welch; October 14, 1786; 200 ac.; on both sides Ireland Creek; joining Mallory John's land.

John McCormick; October ?, 1786; 100 ac.; on the Main Bedford Road; joining Benjamin Hodges, David McCormick and John McCormick.

## Page 57

William Morris; October 17, 1786; 350 ac.; head branches Willis's River joining Capt. John Moseley, John Morris, and David McCormick.

William Morris, Jr.; October 18, 1786; 120 ac.; joining David McCormick, John McCormack, and William Morris.

John Radford; date ? ; 1220 ac.; on big and little Phillips Creek of Slate River and Meredith's Creek; adjoining Little Berry Mosby, James Smith, Archelus Austin, Capt William Perkins, Charles Maxey, Colo. Jos. Cabell's, Road, and William Goff.

## Page 58

John Perkins; October 24, 1786; 220 ac.; on west side Colo. Jos. Cabell's Road on some north branches Little Walton's fork; joining David Pryor's new lines.

George Baskerville; December 14, 1786; 1450 ac.; on both sides Wreck Island Creek including the place called Kennon's Mines; joining Jeremiah Whitney, Mrs. Sarah Berks and new lines.

## Page 59

William Cadberry; December 15, 1786; 1000 ac.; joining Jesse Strange, Widow Pendleton and Kennon's old order of Council survey; on both sides Broad Branch.

George Rice; March 17, 1787; 400 ac.; on both sides Howard's Road joining Israel Winfree, Isaac Sallee, Thomas Asher, James Hundley, Mr. Dobbins, Peter Roy, Joel Drake and Rice's own lines.

Samuel Hale and Charles Gollyhorne; April 7, 1787; 380 ac.; on the Fish Pond Creek; joining Isaac Chandler and new lines.

## Page 60

James McDowal; April 6, 1787; 200 ac.; joining William Maxey and Isaac Chandler.

Nehemiah Evit; April 7, 1787; 400 ac.; on north side Holloway River joining his own land.

William Staton; October 25, 1786; 514 ac.; on Rock Island Creek and each side; joining Colo. Joseph Cabell, Howard's Church road.

## Page 61

German Baker and James Belekes, trustees of Mr. Kennon; June 20, 1788; 4758 ac.; on Fluvanna River and Wreck Island Creek called Kennon's Mine Tract and on Phills Branch; joining Mr. Whitney, Goings, John Burks, John Baskerville, Thomas Ellyson

Henry Bell; November 10, 1784; 12½ ac.; on branches Little Buffalow Creek adjoining James Bristow, Grizzel Coleman old survey, and Mrs. Judith Bell (formerly called the Belmont Tract).

## Page 62

William Allen (son of George H. Allen) (2 tracts) ; October 18, 1786; 214 and 154 acres; on both sides Hunts Creek; latter property of William Allen son of Philip Allen on Hunts Creek; joining William H. Allen, John Flood, Thomas Hardwick and Peter Guerrant.

Thomas Smith; March 10, 1775; on both sides Fish Pond Creek.

Thomas Wood; June 19, 1788; 3½ ac.; north side and adjoining Great Buffalo Creek a branch of Willis River; joining Thomas Randolph, Edward Gibson, and John Moseley,

## Page 63

James Howl; November 16, 1789; 100 ac.; south side and adjoining Slate River; joining John Allen, Tandy Holeman, ---- Amonett, George Beaver, James Howl.

Peter Guerrant; December 10, 1790; 14½ ac.; on north branches Hunts Creek; joining Charles Perrow, Peter David and Peter Guerrant.

John Horsely; June 10, 1785; 52 ac.; on branches Fluvanna River and Bent Creek; joining Mace Freeland, Christian's order, and his own land; Horsely from Amherst County.

Francis Ware Childress; December 21, 1790; 122 ac.; on both sides Buck and Doe Creek a branch of Willis' River; joining Daniel Saunders, John Hooper.

Joshua Fry; November 10, 1791; 33 ac.; bounded by Isaac Berriman and Joshua Fry.

## Page 64

John Pankey; March 25, 1788; 611 ac.; on south side Colo. John Cabell's Court House Road and each side of Old Doe Creek and Matthews Road; joining Colo. John Harris and John Cabell.

Charles Call; September 20, 1788; 122 ac.; on a branch of Hunt Creek; joining Anthony Levilliam, John Flood, Samuel Allen, William Jones and Charles Call.

Charles Maxey; September 29, 1788; 50 ac.; on Main Ireland Creek; joining Henry Rakes survey; transferred to William Rakes.

John Dolling; May 3, 1788; 280 ac.; on an unnamed creek (!); joining John Pankey and John Dolling and James Dolling.

## Page 65

Thomas Staples; June 1, 1789; 100 ac.; joining lines of James Dilliard and Richard Taylor and his own lines.

James Dilliard; June 2, 1789; 220 ac.; joining lines of Thomas Staples, Richard Taylor, Oglesby, Christian, Dilliard.

James Baker; September 29, 1788; 130 ac.; on waters of Ireland Creek.

John Bradley; June 3, 1789; 20 ac.; joining lines of Diuguid and Doss.

Isaac Smith; June 3, 1789; 27 ac.; near Wreck Island Creek; joining Nimrod Reach, William Diuguid, Thomas Stanley, and Isaac Smith.

## Page 66

Peter Moses; June 3, 1789; 60 ac.; joining Joseph Bradley and "lines unknown".

William Diuguid; June 4, 1789; 240 ac.; joining James Patteson, Hite(?) Elkins, and William Diuguid.

John Ford; November 23, 1789; 48 ac.; on a branch of Slate River and joining lines of Nancy Howard, Kid, and the lines of John Ford.

David Kyle; November 25, 1789; 250 ac.; joining Mr. Robert Kyle and David Kyle's own lines.

Page 67

William Thornhill; November 25, 1789; 600 ac.; joining William Thornhill's lines, David Kyle.

James Burnett; November 27, 1789; joining John Patteson Senr., Cooper Brown, James Burnett's own land.

Charles Maxey; December (?) 2, 1789; 450 ac.; joining William Rakes, Joseph Cabell's Road on the west lying on the head of Sycamore Island Creek; note: Joseph Cabell's survey of 2540 acres made 2 day of March 1791 takes 50 acres "part of the above as you see" drawn on plat.

Page 68

John Perkins; December 24, 1789; 400 ac.; west side Colo. Joseph Cabell's road on Sycamore Island Creek joining Charles Maxey and John Perkins; David Pryor. Note: Since making this survey of 400 acres for John Perkins has made two different surveys one for Mr. John Hopkins and the other for Colo. Joseph Cabell which surveys was made by older entries then his and has taken ---- part of his survey as you see above - the 2d March 1791.

Elisha Poor; February 11, 1790; 350 ac.; joining Colo. John Harris, John Cabell and John Stephens; lying east side of Irons Creek.

Flamstead Jones; February 17, 1790; 500 ac.; on head west oak Branch of Rock Island Creek; joining John James and Charles Irving.

Page 69

George Rice; February 17, 1790; 300 ac.; joining John James, Peter Rory and a survey just lately made for Flemstead Jones.
Notes: This survey of 300 acres of land which was surveyed for George Rice is included and taken by Powhatan Bolling. By virtue of a prior Entry; teste Henry Bell Surv. Wherefore no Certificate has ever been granted the said Rice. But since the above was written (vizt:) this 9th day of May 1794. I have granted certificate to the three sons of said George Rice (namely) to Davenport Rice, Edwin Rice and George Rice legatees of the George Rice; Bolling's right of entry being void by law. Henry Bell surv.

Richard Taylor; May 3, 1788; each side of John Dolling and Archiles Austin survey on courthouse road (shown); Mr. Pankey a neighbor.

John Briant; May 17, 1790; 790 ac.; on waters of Rock Island Creek joining lines of Daniel Low's (Mrs) widow, Tapscott, Joseph Cunningham, Harden Perkins, and Mr. Howard; on both sides Howard's road (shown).

## Page 70

James Staton; October 23, 1790; 2150 ac.; on some of south branches of James River being bounded on east by Benjm Howard's road (shown) and on west by Nicholas Cabell's ferry road (shown); joining David Patteson, Joseph Cabell, William Staton, and Charles Irving.

Reuben Staton; October 23, 1790; 200 ac.; joining David Patteson and James Staton; surveyed for Elijah and Isham Staton's orphans of Reuben Staton; a small road shown.

## Page 71

John Suddarth; October 26, 1790; 230 ac.; lying each side Rock Island Creek joining lines of William Staton, John Northcutt, Charles Beazeley, Thomas Anderson, and Colo. Joseph Cabell on road to Warren (shown).

James Couch; date?; 150 ac.; on some of waters of Rock Island Creek; joining Daniel Pucket, Harden Perkins, and William Howard.

Roling Flowers; December 18, 1790; 90 ac.; joining Stephen Garrett, Benjamin Moseley; on courthouse road.

William Goff; December 4, 1790; 11 ac.; on south side and adjoining Slate River bounded by lines of Benjamin Moseley and Nathan Ayres.

John Conner; December 6, 1790; 50 ac.; joining lines of Lee Dolling and Nicholas Conner.

## Page 72

David Patteson; December 2, 1790; 1300 ac.(-559 formerly patented = 741) joining south side Fluvanna River and bounded by Samuel Spencer's lines and Charles Irving, It being inclusive of all his lands the south side of said river; on Nicholas Cabell's ferry road (shown) on Sycamore Island Creek.

Adler Arrington; date?; 900 ac. and 364 ac. (1264) joining lines of James Patteson, William Diuguid and Mayo's old lines; note at bottom "the above joins Thos Still.
## Page 73
Tillotson Parish; December 14, 1790; 150 ac.; including Goodings Church surveyed for the Church Wardens of Tillotson Parish agreeable to an old entry made by the CW of Tillotson parish; adjoining Josias Chambers; Colo. Joseph Cabell; church shown and a creek too.

Joseph Cabell; March 2, 1791; 400 ac.; on Sycamore Island Creek surveyed for

Mr. John Hopkins the 2d day of March 1791 and since transferred to Joseph Cabell Senr by attached order.

Leonard Ballow; March 30, 1790; 1200 ac.; on east fork Sycamore Island Creek joining lines of David Patteson, Joseph Cabell, Charles Maxey, and John Breckenridge; John Hopkins. N. Cabell's road shown.

## Page 74

Colo. John Cabell Esq.; April 14, 1790; 2200 ac.; on Fluvanna River joining lines of George Berks; river shown; Negro Creek shown; Ireland's Creek shown; an island in river shown.

George Birks; April 15, 1791; 1250 ac; joining Colo. John Cabell; Joseph C. Megginson, his own lines; altered October 25, 1816 by John Patteson surveyor.

Colo. William Smith(Chesterfield); April 16, 1791; joining Henry-Rakes (crossed out in original) Mallory Johns (mulatto) George Birks, Colo. John and Joseph Cabell; on Negro Creek and a road show.

## Page 75

Powhatan Bolling; March 23, 1791; 862 ac.; (part of description mutilated); four different surveys on Muddy Creek ---- down Howard's Road and the road leading from Gooding Church to James River Road cross, the beginning of each survey, as specified in the entry's made by the late Colo. Robert Bolling dec'd and bounded by the lines of Colo. Joseph Cabell, William Staton, John Northcutt, John Beazley, James Hundley, George Rice, Taylor and Harrison and the lands of Tillotson Parish; Surveyed for Powhatan Bolling, eldest son and heir-at-law to Robert Bolling dec'd by Cary Harrison ass't; crossroads shown; Tillotson Parish land wedged in by Bollings; first entry 30 ac.; second entry 256 ac.; third entry 176 ac.; fourth entry 400 ac.

Richard Taylor and Cary Harrison; March 23, 1791; 268 ac.; on Muddy Creek and its branches and bounded by lines of Powhatan Bolling, Peter Roy, Samuel Winfree and John Bates; surveyed by Cary Harrison asst to Henry Bell, SBC; shows a creek and Saml Winfree's "drill house".

William Stephens; March 9, 1791; 9 ac.; west side Dry Beaver Pond Creek and bounded by John Ferguson and Thomas Staples and by order of the said Thomas Stephens the works are recorded in the name of his son William Stephens.

## Page 76

John Radford; April 22, 1791; 600 ac; joining Colo. Joseph Cabell's late survey and lines of John Radford.

John Hopkins; April 27, 1791; 400 ac.; each side Sycamore Island Creek joining lines of Colo. Joseph Cabell. Note: transferred to Joseph Cabell.

Jessee Thornhill; May 12, 1791; 28 ac.; adjoining Helton, Horseley, Freeland, and Kennon's Order of Council.

## Page 77

William Thornhill; May 13, 1791; 190 ac.; joining Thomas and John Stephens.

David Kyle; May 13, 1791; 650 ac.; 250 ac. of which were formerly surveyed November 25, 1789; joining lines of John Stephens, William Thornhill, Kyle's own lines, new lines, and Joseph Cabell's survey.

David Pryor; May 17, 1791; 195 ac.; joining Thomas Anderson, John Couch, James Staton, and David Pryor.

John Patteson; May 26, 1791; 150 ac.; joining James Nowling, Charles Layne, Nathan Neighbours, and Patteson's own lines, Mr. Doss; Note: July 8, 1801, This day I have granted the works of this 120 ac. of land by virtue of said John Patteson's warr't of ---- dated 19th May 1801. Note: Buckingham, etc, May the 24th 1799, this day I resurveyed this tract of land and find it contains only 120 acres, signed John Patteson.

## Page 78

Charles Patteson; May 13, 1791; 13 ac.; north side Ripley's Creek joining lines of Richard Ripley, Thomas Miller (dec'd), and Charles Patteson.

William Phelps; May 26, 1791; 380 ac.; east side of Bent Creek; joining lines of William Thornhill, Peggy Long, Samuel Coleman, George Diuguid and William Phelps.

James Smith; November 18, 1791; 388 ac.; on Meredith's Creek joining lines of John Radford, William Perkins, Charles Jones and Little Berry Mosby.

John Stephens; May 26, 1791; 300 ac.; on Irons Creek joining Colo. Joseph Cabell, David Kyle, Elisha Poor and Stephen's own lines.

## Page 79

James Spears; August 24, 1792, 40 ac.; on south side and adjoining Fluvanna River bounded by Widow Freeland and Joseph Cabell Esq.

David Patteson; October 19, 1792; 200 ac.; joining Powhatan Bolling, Thomas Battes and Josias Chambers.

Mac Pendleton; October 25, 1792; 50 ac.; joining Kennon's order of Council, Mr. Allen's and George Helton's.

George Helton; October 23, 1792; 400 ac.; joining lines of Kennon's order of Council, Allen's and Howard's.

## Page 80

John Horseley and Mace Freeland; October 26, 1792; 320 ac.; south side of Fluvanna River and adjoining lines of Horseley and Freeland partly on David's Creek and some of the waters of Bent Creek.

William Cheek; January 22, 1794; 33 ac.; on Bent Creek joining Reuben Curree, John Wright, William Galberry and Cheek's own lines.

John Elgin; May 18, 1793; 260 ac.; joining George Diuguid and John Elgin.

Page 81

William Jones; March 29, 1794; 371 ac.; joining lines of John Jones Senr and John Pittman.

Jos. Brown; April 24, 1794; 93 ac.; joining lines of David Gilliam and Joseph Brown. Note: November 17, 1794, These works were located by a land warrant dated 9th May 1794 ---- 1353 No. 439 and this day granted the said Brown on Cert. for the same by Virtue of the said location.

NOTE: "March the 25th, 1794. All the preceding Surveys made by Mr. John Patteson (one of my assistant surveyors) including this one of Colo. Joseph Cabell's for 14,740 acres are this day settled up and the Ballance due from the said Mr. John Patteson charged in Money in my fee book (rest is cut off).

Page 82

Joseph Brown; April 26, 1794; 260 ac.; joining Josiah McKinney, William Maxey, Capt. David Parrish, James Walker and the lines of Joseph Brown. Note: Nover the 17th, 1794, this survey was located by virtue of the same warrant that his last survey of 93 acres and certificate granted at the same time to the said Brown. signed Henry Bell.

William Morris Jr.; November 24, 1794; 100 ac.; joining lines of widow Gilliam, James Walker and Crouch's. References to assignment to Jno Gilliam and R. Gilliam; on waters of Holloday.

Moses Flood; November 26, 1794; 80 ac.; joining lines of Sherwood McCormack those formerly John Stevens, Judith Godsey, Mr. Green.

Page 83

James Hundley; October 7, 1794; 174 ac.; joining lines of Mr. Phill Duvall, Obediah Smith, Mr. Pleasants and John Christian.

John Booth and Thomas Staples; October 29, 1794; 1500 ac.; joining lines of John Miller, Robert Roggers, Kennon's Order of Council and Thomas Matthews being partly on the waters of Wreck Island Creek and Fluvanna River; Coleman's Road and Whitney's Road shown.

Page 84

John Booth and Thomas Staples; October 28, 1794; 600 ac.; joining of John Miller, Isaac Staples, John Dixon, Capt. John Chambers, and the county line "newly choped," and John Booth partly on little Wreck Island Creek.

John Childres, Edward Morriss, James Childres and Thomas Gregory; January 8, 1795; 224 ac.; adjoining the south side of the Great Road on the waters of Holloday River being bounded by lines of James Walker, John Reuben, and Thomas Gregory.

John Guilliam; January 8, 1795; 48 ac.; adjoining William Morriss, east side adjoining Holloday River; James Walker, Mr. Gilliam's own lines.

Page 85

David Guilliam; January 8, 1795; 460 ac.; on some of the waters of Holloday River joining lines of Joseph Brown, William Morriss Jr., Crouch's, Richard Gilliam, James Walker, David McCormack and Olive Branch a road shown.

Richard Gilliam; January 16, 1795; 261 ac.; joining lines of Robert Smith, Uriah Smith, and Charles Patteson; lying on waters of Slate River.

Jacob Cottrell; May 5, 1795; 78 ac.; joining Anthony Murray, Alexander Banks and Jordan's Road.

Page 86

Reubin Clopton; March 2, 1795; 1000 ac.; joining lines of Gresham Lee and Joel Watkins; "surveyed for Reubin Clopton executor for Robert Clopton deceased."

Reuben Clopton; February 20, 1795; 1000 ac.; joining lines of Michael Jones, Jeffrey Smith, Richard Gilliam and Richard Taylor. Surveyed for Reubin Clopton executor for Robert Clopton deceased. By order this survey is transferred to John Patteson asst. surveyor. October 10, 1795; Pickshin Road shown.

Page 87

William Flowers; March 18, 1795; 370 ac.; joining John Elgins, William Diuguid, Shadrach Smith, Andrew Vassar, Alexander Smith, Andrew Flowers and William Flowers own lines; shows a creek.

Richard North; August 5, 1795; 108 ac. ; joining Thomas Matthews and John Booth and Thomas Staples.

John Radford, September 25, 1795; 56 ac.; joining William Goff, Will Rakes, and Little B. Mosby; on Colo. Joseph Cabell's Road.

Page 88

Colo. Charles Patteson; March 27, 1794; 298½ ac.; on both sides Phelp's Branch joining lines of William Phelps, John Pankey, Edward Patteson and George Diuguid. Surveyed by J. Watkins asst. surv.

Thomas Chancellor; April 2, 1794; 71 3/4 ac.; southwest side Naked Mountain joining his own old lines and James Patteson and Peter Patteson.

Richard Gilliam; February 25, 1795; 241 3/4 ac.; on both sides a fork of Willis's River joining William Morris Sr., Thomas Blackburn, James Routon, and Epaphroditus Gilliam dec'd; surveyed for Richard Gilliam (son and heir at law of the said Epaphroditus Gilliam dec'd) February 25, 1795; shows river.

### Page 89

Richard Gilliam, son of Epaphroditus Gilliam; March 13, 1795; 413 3/4 ac.; on branches Slate River; joining William Morris Sr., Olive Branch, Robert Smith and John Webb.

Gresham Lee; February 26, 1795; 63 ac.; on branches Willis's River joining lines of Thomas Grigory, Thomas Blackburn, William Morris Sr., Edward Morris, and James Walker (son of Henry).

Peter Patteson; January 28, 1795; 91 ac.; near branches of Appomattox River joining John Patteson, his own lines, and Moses Sweney.

### Page 90

Peter Patteson; May 7, 1795; 156 ½ ac.; on branches Appomattox River joining Thomas Trent, Samuel Staples, Henry Flood, and William Webb Jr.

Peter Patteson; May 7, 1795; 43 ¼ ac.; on south side Naked Mountain joining Turpin's lines, James Patteson and Thomas Chancellor.

James Walker (son of Henry); October 17, 1792; 482 ac.; on waters of Holliday River and on both sides Buckingham Road joining Hodge's old tract, John Gilliam Gilliam (son of William Gilliam dec'd), John Walker dec'd, John Childress, Thomas Grigory and William Morris Jr.

### Page 91

James Walker (son and heir of Henry Walker dec'd); October 19, 1792; 295 ac.; on south side Holliday and on both sides Branch called Walkers Spring Branch joining William Gilliam dec'd and John Walker (son and heir at law of John Walker dec'd); shows creek.

Joseph Brown; October 23, 1792; 434 3/4 ac.; on both sides Walker's Spring Branch joining his old lines and lines of Ollive Branch and James Walker (son of John Walker dec'd).

Land office treasury warrant number 2195 for George Billups and George Carson for 356 ½ac. due Billups and Carson in exchange for part of Land Office exchange treasury warrant number 1342, issued the 16th of November 1802; dated March 8, 1814; signed, ---- Hargrove; note: "This must be returned to the office by April Court 1814".

### Page 92

Josiah Giles; March 20, 1793; 290 ac.; on each side Fishpond Creek and on both sides Beards and Burnett's roads joining Edward Patteson, Richard Taylor

Charles Gallahorn and Samuel Staples; part of survey is missing.

Josiah McKenny; March 20, 1793; 160 ac.; on both sides Walkers Spring Branch joining James McDowel and Joseph Brown; shows creek.

Part of a survey, for whom it is not clear; note attached: "Report of High Court of Chancery if not recorded to be done without delay; recorded and exd in platt book. Shows part of a survey beginning at Wreck Island Creek in Fluvanna River joining Thomas Thornhill, William Bradley, Mrs. Freeland, David Kyle; no date. Added note: "reverse of 227".

## Page 93

Peter Patteson; March 6, 1793; 375 ac.; on branches Fishpond and Wolfs Creek and on both sides of Burnett's road and joining Joel Ferguson Gresham Lee, Charles Gallahan and Josiah Giles; shows a road.

William Webb Jr.; March 9, 1793; 168 ½ ac.; branches Wolf Creek a fork of Appomattox River joining William Coffee, Robert Ferguson, his own lines, John Patteson, and Thomas Trent.

John Webb; October 10, 1792; 400 ac.; on branches of Slate River and on both sides Buckingham Road.

## Page 94

Thomas Cobbs (J.R.) 717 ac. on each side Rock Island Creek joining John Briant, James Couch, Pucketts, Thomas Carter and Capt. Thomas Anderson. December 9, 1795; Mr. Howard and vacant land adjoining; Warrants sent with works. Exchange: Warrant granted to Joshua Gibson for 283 ac. number 481 and dated October 20 1792. Warrant granted to Jno. Davidson for 300 ac. number 482 and date October 27, 1792.

John Falwell; 100 ac.; joining James Couch, Darbe Bondurant and Joseph Cunningham and Mrs. Tapscott. December 11, 1795. Warrant sent with works; warrant granted to Charles Cottrell the 11th June 1783 for 1309½ ac. number 16,763.

Nathaniel Maxey; January 2, 1796; 300 ac.; joining Couch, Walker and widow Gilliam; Warrant granted to Mary Maxey the 10th of September 1782 for 1075 ac. number 14,167; on a branch of Holladay River.

## Page 95

William Griggory; March 7, 1796; 23 ac.; joining Williams Jones Jr. and William Griggory. Warrant granted to Moses Sweeny for 1000 ac. dated 7th October 1782.

Lineus Bolling; 392 ac.; joining John Epperson, John Hooper, Francis Ware Childress, Thomas Woldrige and George Carter on the west side Buck and Doe Creek; March 22, 1796; Warrant sent with works; Warrant granted to Bernard Markham dated 1st March 1782 for 5000 ac., number 11,174.

Armistead Garnett; 118 ac. joining Mr. Loyd, John Epperson, George Carter, John Childress and Thomas Truman Murphy; March 25, 1796; warrant sent with works; warrant granted to John Bernard the 15th November 1782 for 618 3/4 ac., number 14,838. This survey was originally surveyed for ---- Miller and by him transferred to Armistead Garnett.

## Page 96

Joseph Payne; 1000 ac.; waters of Evats (?) Creek joining lines of one Maddox, Gresham Lee, and Samuel Watkins; surveyed for Joseph Payne assignee of John Barnes 22 April 1796; on Burnett's Road and another unnamed road.

George Nicholas; December 1, 1796 joining George Nicholas on the north and west, Robert Blanks on the east and new lines on the South.

George Nicholas; December 19, 1796; 167 ac.; on James River joining George Nicholas on west, James River on north, Robert Blank on east and new lines on south; shows river.

William Hansford; August 19, 1794; on both sides Phelp's Creek joining John H. Cock dec'd, Robert Blanks, John Fearn dec'd and William Kidd.

William McGraw; December 19, 1796; 29 ac.; on waters Willis' Creek joining Samuel Sanders and George Carrington dec'd.

## Page 97

William McCraw; 43 ac.; surveyed for McCraw on January 23, 1796; on both sides Willis's River and Buck and Doe Creek in the said county by virtue of a warrant for 806 ac. of land number 12,234 dated the 10th June 1782. Granted to Walter Nunnalle. Assigned by him to Francis Walthall and by him the said Walthall to the said William McCraw; by Cary Harrison asst for Henry Bell; bounded as per plat above: shows river and creek; joining Thomas Wooldridge, Daniel Sanders, John Sanders. Works delivered to T. Wood ye 28 December 1796.

Simon Huddlestone; 252 ac.; on main branch of Hatcher's Creek and on both sides Bells Court house road adjacent Joseph Carter, Francis Moseley, Samuel LeSeuer, James Welch, Rolfe Eldridge, and Henry Grizzle; January 31, 1799. This survey being made within the Patent lands of Robert Thompson the works are suppressed.

Joseph Evans; 69 ac.; on a small east branch of Turpins Creek adjoining lines of William Newton, Chastain LeSeuer and Rolfe Eldridge. Surveyed for Evans in two surveys, the first made the 19th February 1796, the second made the 21st February 1797. Warrants delivered with the works to Eliza. Evans wife to the said Joseph the 10th January 1798.

## Page 98

John Miller; 1300 ac.; 2 surveys; on both sides Hatcher's Creek, Horn Quarter Road and Buckingham Branch; October 31, 1796. Henry Cary dec'd, William A. Fry. Mrs. Judith Bell; "this line part of John Gresham's patent land sold by Archd Cary dec'd to Robert Anderson;

line of Henry Cary dec'd for his Willis's River survey extends farther
southerly in the same direction to the extent of 100? poles.

Henry Rawlins; 311 ac.; on both sides little Buffaloe Creek a small north
branch of Willis's River in 2 surveys, March 7, 1797; creek shown;
Alexander Mitchell and George Adcock, Anderson Adcock, Henry Bell,
Mrs. Bell's line called Belmont Tract, Patrick O'Briant dec'd, Thomas
Christian dec'd.

## Page 99

John Miller; 400 ac.; joining John Wright, Samuel Coleman, Elizabeth
Evans old line, James Christian, John Miller, Surveyed originally
for ---- on the 30th May 1760 and since relocated by Miller for
whom the works have been ---- 22d November 1793 and again surveyed
November 1796.

Robert Cary; 296 ac.; on both sides ---- Road on south draughts of Brook
---- a branch of Willis's River and joining Joshua Nicholas, Jesse
Garland, Jno. Vest and Robert Cary's; August 30, 1796.

---- sworn chain carriers ---- on his own and Nicholas' Line 4°
----on all the others 3°

Price Perkins; 666 ac.; April 1797; on both sides Great George Creek and
joining John Briant, William Anglin; Randolph Jefferson, Price Perkins,
and vacant lands.

## Page 100

Crossed out survey for Francis Ware Childress for 122 acres; note says
already recorded on page 63 (which it is).

Powhatan Bolling; 24 ac.; May 10, 1791; on both sides Mountain Creek one
of Main branches of Willis's River and bounded by lines of Archibald
Cary dec'd and Samuel Ridgeway dec'd.

Powhatan Bolling; 38 ac.; upon the Rocky Ridge; bounded by William Mallory,
the suppositious lines of John Nelson and Powhatan Bolling. May 18, 1791.

John McCoseley; 200 ac.; on branches Slate River bounded by lines of Capt.
Charles and John ---- (date and rest torn off); part of survey torn off.

## Page 101

Isaack Garrett; 303 ac.; on both sides Troublesome Creek a branch of Slate
River joining William Fugua, Henry Flood, David Flowers, John and Cliff
Hazlewood, and Isaack Garrett; April 14, 1791; shows creek.

Thomas Gibson; 200 acres on meanders of Appomattox River joining Abednago
Boaz and Arther Conner, Thomas Trent, and William Coffee. Note: "This
platt has been thro' mistake bein again recorded in folio 118."

Joel Watkins; 134 ac.; branches Appomattox River adjoining Joseph Calland (dec'd) and Joel Watkins for whom the survey was made by transfer from his brother Silas Watkins (heirs at law of Joel Watkins dec'd) on 5th May 1791.

Page 102

William Cofey (Goffey also on plat); 203 ac.; branches Appomattox River joining Gilbert North, Robert Ferguson, Philip Matthews, Thomas Trent, and Thomas Gibson; May 4, 1791.

Richard Lee; 290 ac.; on both side Fishpond Creek, a branch of Appomattox River and on both sides Burnetts road and joining to Beards road and bounded by lines of Edward Patteson, Richard Taylor, Thomas Smith, and Samuel Staples, ---- of May 1791; shows creek.

Gresham Lee; 800 ac.; waters of Wolf and Fishpond Creeks branches of Appomattox River and bounded by Lee's own land and new lines; May 3, 1791.

Page 103

William Allen (son of Geo.); 300 ac.; on waters of Hunt's Creek, adjoining lines of John Marshall, the Furnace land, Capt. William Allen and Sharrens(?) tract; January 2, 1797. This survey was made by virtue of James Hudnett's location dated the 26th January 1793 and transferred to William Allen son of George Allen. Surveyed by William R. Bernard, assistant surveyor.

Charles Perrow; 41 ac.; adjoining lines of Perrow, a new line, Samuel Jordan, and Henry White, January 13, 1797. Warrant sent to the Register with Armistead Garnetts survey of 118 ac.

William Allen (son of George Hunt Allen); 14 ac.; adjoining lines of Terry Galloway, William H. Allen, Jacob Agee and William H. Allen (again) assignee of James Hudnett; date?

William Allen; 104 ac.; adjoining John Flood, Capt. William Allen on waters of Hunts Creek, surveyed for Capt William Allen 24 December 1796. Warrant in name of Holloway Hadgins for 622½ ac. dated 15 November 1782, number 14,836 - sent to Register's Office with this survey.

Page 104

Terry Galloway; 100 ac.; adjoining William H. Allen, Lawhorne's tract, and Robert Easley; 29 December 1796; tract called "Musket and Bayonet" because of odd shape.

John Miller; June 21, 1796; 48 ac.; adjoining Mr. Joshua Nicholas=Vest (?!) and Abner Seay; surveyed by Joseph Roper.

Joshua Nicholas; August 17, 1796; 10 ac.; joining Colo. George Hooper and Nicholas' own land.

## Page 105

Richard Bondurant; 130 ac.; joining Gad Blankenship, ---- Maxey, and Elijah Howle; October 4, 1797.

Lineus Bolling; July 18, 1797; 352 ac.; joining Mr. Craig, Alexander Banks, Nunalleys and Bolling's own land.

John Pittman; July 15, 1797; 300 ac.; on Murphy's road joining James Wilson, Patrick O'Brian, John Moseley (dec'd), John Hooper, and John Epperson.

## Page 106

Capt. John Saunders; July 31, 1797; acres?; each side Willis's River, bounded by lines of Saunders.

Darbe Bondurant; October 3, 1797; 143½ ac.; joining Mrs. Tapscott, John Winfrey and Darbe Bondurant's own lines.

Capt. Thomas Anderson; July 26, 1797; 600 ac.; in fork of Rock Island Creek joining lines of Mrs. Tapscott, Edwin Rice, Thomas Ray Woods, James Staton, Thomas Cobb and Thomas Anderson's lines. Error that on the 9th day of July 1801 I have resurveyed this tract of land and find it to contain 200 acres belonging to Simon Hudson. Works issued for 400 acres - by John Patteson.

## Page 107

David Patteson; February 7, 1797; 44 ac.; each side Arthur's Creek and joining lines of John Breckenridge, Charles Anderson and lines of David Patteson. Note: new works is granted to David Patteson for the above land having date the 12th day of June 1799, old one cancelled. Warr. gone with works to Registers office.

John Pittman; November 1795; 132 ac.; joining Judith Godsey, John Hooper, Capt. Samuel Saunders, Lynch's, east side of John's Court House Road.

Edmund Page; 236 ac.; surveyed for Page by virtue of James Page's location made the 7th of February 1797 and by the said James ordered to be surveyed in the name of said Edmund... in head spring of Turpin's Creek and on Fry's Branch, a branch of Willis's river adjoining line of Thompson's old patent land, Rolfe Eldridge, James Welch and Edward Walton (formerly Fry's) lines; October 25, 1797.

## Page 108

Daniel Woodson and John Cheadle (?); 320 ac.; north branches Appomattox River adjoining lines of Richard Peak, Claybourn Maddox, James Walker, Jacob Woodson and Joel Watkins; August 3, 1797; surveyed by Cary Harrison; on Walker's road and Ceaser's (?) Spring Branch and Ransoms Spring Branch. (This was the first entry for Cary Harrison as surveyor).

Thomas Bondurant; February 22, 1798; 4 ac.; joining Jacob Agee, a tract formerly granted to Stephen Ford, and William H. Allen.

Mary Allen; February 22, 1798; 50 ac.; on water's of Green's Creek adjoining Capt. William Allen, Peter Guerrant and vacant land.

Mary Allen; February 21, 1798; 34 ac.; waters of Hunt's Creek adjoining lands of William H. Allen and Jacob Agee; "called the pick ax"; also joining William B. Bernard's assignees.

Peter Guerrant; February 21, 1798; 45 ac.; on Hunt's Creek adjoining Jacob Agee and Guerrant's own land; Warrant sent to Register's office with William Gregory's survey of 23 ac.

Peter Guerrant; February 22, 1798; 100 ac.; waters of Green's Creek adjoining Capt. William Allen, William H. Allen, Robert Easley and vacant land. Warrant returned with William Gregory's survey of 23 acres.

## Page 109

Peter Guerrant; February 21, 1798; 300 ac.; on Rocky Creek adjoining Henry White, Samuel Jordan dec'd, Stephen Ford dec'd Jacob Agee and Guerrant's own land.

John Harris; April 13, 1798; 142 ac.; waters Crooked Creek adjoining lands of Matthew Ayres, Jacob Duncan, Daniel Guerrant, Joseph Harris, George Rye and Harris' own land.

Rane Chastain (son of Peter); April 27, 1798; 68 ac.; on water's Green's Creek surveyed for Chastain; adjoining lands of George Ryes (?), Agee, William Allen and Chastain's own land.

William Allen; April 27, 1798; 50 ac.; on waters of Greens Creek adjoining lands of Mary Allen, vacant land, and Allen's own land.

Kincaid and Wilson; Ma--- 15, 1798; 2 ac.; including Kincaid and Wilson's store house, adjoining Martha Branch and Robert Kincaid.

Survey for 10 acres adjoining Robert Kincaid, new lines, Matthew Branch and Kincaid and Wilson on May 15, 1798. Warrant returned with John Millers survey of 48 acres dated June 21, 1796.

## Page 110

Matthew Wilson; 47 ac.; on waters Slate River adjoining lines of Matthew Branch, James Wilson and new lines; May 15, 1798; Note: May 19, 1798, this day settled with William R. Bernard for the foregoing surveys made by him as my assistant, amounting in the whole to twenty one surveys and for which I have received my full proportion together with the Colledge fees for the same. And passed my receipt in full for ₤19.6.3 July 31, 1798. This day made out a list of all the foregoing surveys since the 31st day of July last and returned to the ---- Office of this county acoording to law.

Richard Gilliam (son of Epaphroditus) 232 ac.; January 5, 1798 agreeable to an order of Court bearing date of December Court 1797 and directed

to the surveyor of the county aforesd or his deputy and is joining
the lines of the Widow Johns, Samuel Saunders, Epaphraditus Gilliams,
William Morriss, Thomas Blackburn and James Routen.
Note: from some error in the first certificate a new one is granted
to Richard Gilliam for the said quantity of 232 acres with all its
corners agreeable to the above Platt which certificate bears date
the 10th day of April 1800.

## Page 111

Jacob Sallee; 125 ac.; on Briants Creek and Court House road joining the
land of William Gipson and Frances Harriss; December 15, 1797; warrant
gone with R. Bondurant's survey for 130 ac.;

Thomas Hall; 150 ac.; November 1797; on Shapr's Creek joining Capt. Anthony
Murry and Beaber (?).

David Bondurant; January 12, 1797; 43 ac.; on ridges near Sharp's Creek
joining lines of Capt. Anthony Murrey, Jacob Cottrell and Mrs. Tapscott.

## Page 112

John Miller; May 11, 1798; 84 ac.; under the north side of Willis's Mountain
joining Joshua Nicholas and the widow McLoyd; warrant gone to Register's
office with his survey for 300 acres.

Michael Jones; May 10, 1798; 37 ac.; each side Slate River joining lines of
Charles Moseley, Thomas Moseley, David Bell and Micael Jones.

Capt. Jno. Harris; June 8, 1812; 13½ ac.; joining lines of Joseph Burks,
George Christian, Shadrach Smith and "others" on each side of Bent
Creek Road; surveyed by Nelson Patteson.

John Maxey; May 19, 1798; 307 ac.; adjoining Nathl Burton, Edward Maxey,
Charles May, Gad Blankenship, Richard Bondurant and Elijah Howle;
on Goodwin's Road.

## Page 113

Robert Craig; April 21, 1798; 160 ac.; on big George's Creek bounded on one side
side by the road leading from the mouth of Slate River to Albemarle
Old Court House (Scottsville) ferry and otherwise by Robert Craig.
Note: This survey was made under Isham Richardson's warrant for 1402
acres of land number 18007 and by survey assigned down to Craig and
warrant retd with works.

Thomas Bondurant; September 21, 1798; 161 ac.; each side Willis's River
joining lines of Capt Samuel Saunders, Moses Flood, Gran Berry Green,
and Richard Gilliam. Note: Resurveyed December 6, 1817 - metes and
bounds show Moses Flood, Saunders, Gilliam; only 131 acres.

Clabourn Maxey; November 27, 1797; 234 3/4 ac.; joining young Mr. Thomas
Wright, David Bell, Wade, John Dolling and Maxey as assignee of
Thomas Matthews.

## Page 114

Benjamin and David Bondurant; September 18, 1798; 120 aa.; head of south fork of Rock Island Creek and each side of the road leading from Goodwin's Church to Albemarle Old Court House (Scottsville) Ferry joining Joseph Goode, Isaac Sallee, Fore, and Darbe Bondurant. surveyed by (?) Rich Rice.

Samuel Taylor; September 15, 1798; 28 ac.; on James Benning Spring Branch joining a tract of land known by Martin's lines, James Benning's lines and Taylor.

Edward Philbottes; September 24, 179-; 160 ac.; on ridges between Turpin's Creek and Slate River joining lines of Samuel Taylor, Mrs. Holeman, James Howle, George Braber (?), and Jacob Chalton for Philbottes; a note is illegible.

## Page 115

Hercules Agee; December 15, 1798; 12 ac.; on south side and adjoining Slate River bounded by river, Isaac Sallee and Agee. Note: Prior to this (to wit) on the 21st March 1789 this land was surveyed but the works running out of date with cause that it is again surveyed - teste Henry Bell

Samuel Watkins; December 24, 1798; 171 ac.; on north side of Appomattox River and joining said river, bounded thereby on the south Joel Watkins, Jacob Woodson and James Walker Sen.

Price Perkins; November 23, 1798; 355 ac.; joining Capt. Anthy Murray, Joseph Cunningham, the Widow Tapscott and lines of Price Perkins.

## Page 116

Charles Maxey; April 17, 1799; 520 ac.; joining Colo. John Cabell, Nicholas Vanse Taverns (Smith), John West, John Radford, Joseph Cabell, and John Bagby. Note: By virtue of Charles Howls Warr. for 1884 ac. 200 ac. is surveyed and by Ben Maxeys Warr. for 1000 ac. the bals. of 320 acres is surveyed. This first warr. sent with Jno Radfords inclusive survey for 1820 ac. and the last warr. sent with this survey. Note: These works being stayed for sundry causes until this day, when all matters being duly adjusted they are considered as bearing date only this 24th day of April 1800. Teste Henry Bell.

William Spencer; May 20, 1799; 40 ac.; on each side of a large branch of Slate River joining David Bell, John Hardiman and William Spencer.

## Page 117

William Moseley; May 21, 1799; 180 ac.; joining Capt. John Mosely decd, William Morris, Richard Gilliam, Jeffrey Hardiman Smith and William Moseley. Note: Survey made by virtue of two warrants (vizt) 50 ac. by Ber? Markhams for 5000 ac. No. 11,174 and dated 1 March 1782 and

130 ac. by virtue of Michael Jones's warrant for 200 ac. No. 1734 and dated 19 December 1795. Both of which warrants are gone to Registear's Office.

Phill Bailey; May 11, 1799; 33 ac.; joining John Harriss, Pendleton, Charles Payne and Ben Bailey.

Cary Harrison; June 15, 1796; 200 ac.; joining John Moseley decd, Charles Moseley; on Capt. C. Moseley's rolling road.

### Page 118

Nicholas Vann Tavern; June 18, 1799; 100 ac.; north side Megginson road and John Cabell, and lines of Nicholas Vann Tavern. Note: January 12, 1802 courses and distances of Megginsons's ferry road is as follows and is certified to the Register of Land Office vizt (gives lengthy metes and bounds). Note: These works were made by virtue of two warrants (vizt) first by virtue of a Warrant granted to Charles Cattrell for 1309½ acres No. 16,763; 50 acres was surveyed and the other 50 acres by virtue of transfer from Jas Agee Assignee of Jno Agee by a warr. for 600 acres No. 2,100 and dates 9 January 1797 and with the last warr. these works are set to Registrar Office.

Thomas Gipson; May 4, 1791; 200 ac.; Appomattox River and William Coffee, Thomas Trent, Abednego Boaz and Arthur Conner.

Francis McCraw; March 19, 1799; 60 ac.; on waters of Willis's River; warrant went with William McCraws survey for 43 acres; adjoining Flood, Green Berry Green, Gilliams old lines.

### Page 119

Cary Harrison; May 5, 1791; 1717 ac.; south side and adjoining Beard's road on north side; Edward Patteson, John Webb and Richard Lee; surveyed for Mr. Richard Taylor (and who transferred the same to Cary Harrison on Fish Pond Creek).

Capt. Charles Moseley; April 12, 1791; 441 ac.; (deduct 68 for M. Jones = 373 ac.); waters of Slate River and on both sides Pick Shin Road; bounded by William Flowers, John Hardiman, David Bell, Michael Jones and Charles Moseley.

### Page 120

Captn Randolph Jefferson; June 18, 1799; 1327 ac.; adjoining Fluvannah River and Big George's Creek and Hardin Perkins, Price Perkins, Mr. Murrey, Robert Craig and Captn. Randolph Jefferson. Shows road leading to ferry (to Scottsville). Note: 1242 acres of this Survey was made by Isham Richardson's warrent for 1402 acres No. 18,007 and 85 acres by Robert Craigs warrant for 160 acres No. 2,437 which last warr: is returned with these works the former one having been sent before to Reg. Off.

Grigory Gannaway; October 27, 1790; 590 acres (deduct 311 for James Johns = 287 acres); branches Appomattox River and bounding Charles Lwelling, William Johns, Peter Hales, John Routon, William Fore and James Crews; shows division lines.

Page 121

John Patteson, asst. surv.; 1000 ac.; June 18, 1799; each side Big Georges Creek and Marrs Road joining Randolph Jefferson, Price Perkins, Mr. Murrey's and Robert Craig.

Note: July 31, 1799; This day made out a list of all the surveys returned and recorded since the 31st day of July 1798, and made return thereof to the Clks office of this County, according to law. Test Henry Bell.

John Briant (son of William); 126 ac.; both sides Middle River of Slate River adjoining Briant Dolling, Nicholas Conner and Thomas Head (decd) surveyed by virtue of Stephen Pankeys warrent for 693 acres No. 16,542 and dated 20 May 1783; October 19, 1799. Note: June 27, 1801: This day Bryant assig. of Samuel McCormick who was asgn of John Cabell ---- returned for this land and I have under virtue of said entry --- him the works of the same wherefore it was not retd by ---- warrant as may be seen in my entry book No. 90. John Patteson.

Page 122

Thomas Word; January 15, 1800; 78 ac.; on Hoopers Road; on sundry small branches Briants Creek, a branch of Glovers Creek which is a branch of Slate River; bounded by lines of Robert Kincaid (in curtesy of his last --------- (missing) wife Mary Cox) John Gibson, William Gibson, and Thomas Word (himself); by virtue of his location, bearing date 16 April 1798 for 100 acres. Warr: gone (vizt) Henry Bell's Exchange Warr: with this works.

John Gipson; July 12, 1799; 73 ac.; joining Matthew Branch's lines, Matthew Wilson, Robert Kincaid, William Gipson, and lines of John Gipson (himself).

William Foree; April 30, 1800; 16 ac.; near Appomattox River joining lines of Joyn Routen and William Foree, P. Edward. Warrent gone with works.

Edmund Winston; March 12, ----; 38 ac.; lines of Edmund Winston, William Greggory and the land formerly Mrs. (mutilated) surveyed for Thomas Walke. By an assignment from John Ferguson. Warrant gone with works.

Page 123

Joseph Robertson; April 14, 1791; 200 ac.; branches of Slate River taking in a small part of Goodings Church Road and bounded by one line of Nathaniel Barton; Note: this was all of page 123, the others on this page were loose papers stuck in.

This platt containing 14,740 acres of land surveyed for Colonel Joseph Cabell was this day compaired and examined by me this 25th day of

March 1794. NO PLATT, just this note; Teste Henry Bell, Surv. BC.

Thomas Livsey; no date; 1000 ac.; Thomas Wright 232 ac.; Thomas Smith 325 ac.; Thomas Matthew's lines; Dry Beaver Pond Creek; partial plat with no notes.

George Carson and George Billups; May 4, 1814; 140 ac.; by virtue of their location on Exchange Land Office Treasury Warrant of 356½ acres and No. 2195 dated March 8, 1814 and bounded as followeth: vizt: beginning at Gresham Lee's and George Carson's Corner, .... Capt. George Perkins line.... line of Joseph Watkins .... aforesaid Lee's line....

Partial plat showing: Nicholas Conner 504 ac.; William Briant 126 ac.; ---- Amos 518 ac.; Francis Amos line; nothing else shown. May go with plat on page 124.

Page 124

Platt of 11,720 acres on David's Creek and its branches on Slate River and its branches, Dry Beaver Pond Creek and its branches and some of the head branches of Fish Pond Creek and including the south end of Slate River Mountain from Thomas Matthew's Road; and bounded by Pick Shin Road, and the lines of Captn Charles Moseley, John Hardiman, Joseph Scott, Francis Amos, Nicholas Conner, James and John Doram, John Pankey, Colo. John Harris, Thomas Matthews, Henry Morris, the two John Browns, James Wells, Isham Brown and Edward Patteson, including a number of tracts of land, some patented and others of a prior claim (vizt): Thomas Moseley's, Joshua Taylors, Connelley Mullins, James Boyd, Thomas Smith, William Briant, Nicholas Conner, Francis Spencer, Thomas Wright, Farrel McFadden, and William Amos; Surveyed for David Bell September 12, 1798 by Cary Harrison asst to Henry Bell.

Page 125

William McCraw; October 6, 1800; 75 ac.; adjoining Thomas Wood, Thomas Woolridge, and Joseph Adcock and Hunter and Epperson the west side and on Appomattox River.

Peter Patteson; October 27, 1800; 108 ac.; on branches of ---- Creek joining lines of Joseph May = Collins, John Fergeson and Joel Fergeson; Surveyed December 10, 1799 by Joel Watkins asst to Henry Bell. Works issued with the warrt; annexd the 27th October 1800 by John Patteson.

John Brothers; October 27, 1800; 50 ac.; joining John Elgin, William Creasey and John Brothers (himself).

Page 126

William Flowers; no date; 44 ac.; joining John Elgin, Joseph ----(mutilated), Brothers, William Creasey and William Flowers (himself).

James Flowers; October 17, 1800; 1 ac.; joining William and Andrew Flowers. Plat and certif. granted to John Henderson for this one acre the 10th

June 1831. Neighbors: John Isbill, Benjamin Abotts, Mrs. Penn.

John Horseley; October 22, 1800; 150 ac.; joining lines of legatees of Alexander Smith decd and the Dancey Dunkards; surveyed for John Horseley who acknowledged to me that Jesse Doss was in Partnership in said survey.

Robert Rodgers; October 23, 1800; 160 ac.; joining lines of Dancey Dunkard, John Horseley and Jesse Doss and lines of Robert Rodgers. Note: May 31, 1802 this day there is 10 acres of this survey turned out by the direction of Robert Rodgers and works granted for only 150 acres by Virtue of Land Office Treasury Warrant: granted to Willis Wills to Henry R. Snead who asgd it to John Patteson who assd it to Jo(?) Rodgers which said warrant was for 150 acres and No. 3183 dated June 17, 1801. Wreck Island Creek noted.

Page 127

Thomas Ellyson and Jarrat E. Taylor; December 30, 1800; 190 ac.; Waters Wreck Island Creek joining lines of Andrew Flowers the legatees of Alexr Smith decd, John Tuggle and Robert Rodgers surveyed for Thomas Ellyson and Jarrat E. Taylor.

William Smith; January 1, 1801; 64 ac.; each side Mirus (?) Creek joining lines of Jesse Smith, Jonas Jones, John Ferguson and Samuel Spencer. Surveyed for William Smith by virtue of his location on an exchange warrant.

David Bondurant; January 27, 1801; 21 ac.; joining lines of James Bartlet Couch, Ann Moss (mulatto) and Tapscott; by virtue of Robert Craigs ---- Office Treasury War:.

Page 128

Robert Craig; January 27, 1801; 7 ac.; joining lines of Randolph Jefferson, William O. Murrey, and Robert Craig.

Carter Page; 1200 ac.; by entry two warrants (600 acres each) dated June 30, 1796 and surveyed the 10th December as above 1796; the said land with 120 acres was surveyed for John Miller October 31, 1796 by entry dated the 15th August 1791 by warrant for 5000 acres entered for 1000 of the same by Cary Harrison. Shows" Horn Quarter Road, stake near (Mays') alias Buckingham branch; Henry Carys Willis's Swamp in joining the other survey of 3942 acres at (A) patented running round to (B); Hatchers Creek runs through the land for (P) to (B); Patented land of John Gresham not claimed by Carter Page bought by Robert Anderson of Colo Archd Cary dec'd; Note: February 10, 1801, The Above platt and certificate was this day presented to me by Carter Page for the purpose of being ----ded and at his request I have ----. I do further certify that Cary Har---- was on the 10th day of Decr 1796 assistant surv. for Henry Bell who was Principal surveyor of Buckingham County. Test John Patteson Surv.

Page 129

Willis Wills; June 26, 1801; 220 ac.; joining lines of James Walker,. Daniel Moseley, Stephen Fuqua, John Routen, John Childress and Nathaniel Maxey.

Dougald Ferguson; June 24, 1801; 90 ac.; on a small mountain joining lines of John Day and Dougald Ferguson.

John Pankey; June 24, 1801; 13 ac.; on each side of the road leading to Bear (?) Creek and joining lines of Edward Patteson and ----Boatwright.

Thomas Anderson; July 9, 1801; 50 ac.; each side of Irving's ferry road joining lines of Thomas Anderson decd and Charles Irving decd; surveyed for the executors of Thomas Anderson to wit Robert Rives, Nathl Anderson and John Harris for the benefit of the legatees of Thomas Anderson.

Page 130

Thomas Anderson decd; July 10, 1801; 162 ac.; nearly all the lower side of Rock Island Creek surveyed for Robert Revis, Nathl Anderson and John Harris exrs of Thomas Anderson decd for the benefit of the devisees of said Thomas Anderson decd.  Note: 15 acres taken out 22 October 1805 agreeable to the last will and testament of Capt Thomas Anderson decd and added to the tract of 235 ac and Hills 150 making in all 400 acres which the said Thomas Anderson willed to his late wife now Mrs. Birks. Adjoining Thomas Anderson's lines, Widow Tapscot; John Briant, Thomas Cobbs.

Thomas Anderson decd; 200 acres on east side of Rock Island Creek surveyed for Robert Revis, Nathl Anderson, and John Harris exors of Thomas Anderson decd for benefit of the devisees of Thomas Anderson decd. Adjoining John Briant, Thomas Cobbs, Price Perkins and Jas Couch.

Thomas Anderson, dec'd; 400 ac.; (note see page 46 of old page numbers); surveyed for Robert Revis, Nathl Anderson, and John Harris for Thomas Anderson decd for the benefit of the devisees of Thomas Anderson decd. This platt of 400 acres is included in a plat on page 46 (?) surveyed 9 July 1801, signed John Patteson. Adjoining James Staton, Simon Hudson, Thomas Anderson, Thos Cobbs, Widow Tapscot, Edwin Rice, Thos Ray.

Page 131

Edward Patteson; July 24, 1801; 12 ac.; joining his own lines and John Pankey.

Benjamin Maxey; August 25, 1800; 600 ac.; lines of Cabell, Harris, David Bell and John Ferguson; Megginson's ferry road, T. Matthews road, Old Doe (?) Creek shown.

John Pankey; 331 acres each side of a creek called the Old Doe the south side and adjoining to Megginson's ferry road bounded by the lines of

David Bells Order of Council and John Ferguson line; surveyed for
John Pankey 20 May 1801.

## Page 132

William Thornhill; July 22, 1801; 650 ac.; joining lines of William Phelps,
John Coleman, John B. Gothard, David Kyle and William Thornhill for
whom the survey was made.

Absolum Thornhill; July 24, 1801; 76 ac.; joining lines of John Elgun,
John Brothers, and Saml Coleman.

Absolum Thornhill; July 23, 1801; 3 ac.; joining John Wright, Robert
Coleman, John Coleman and James Wrights lines.

## Page 133

Hugh McCormick; 133 ac.; March 27, 1801; joining lines of David Bell and
John Pankey's old survey. Note: July 28 these works ---- (resurveyed?)
and issued 124 acres by contract between Cabell and McCormick.

John Cabell; 33 ac.; March 27, 1801; joining lines of John Bagby and John Cabell.

Crossed out plat; says it is on page 132; no names given.

Colo. John Cabell; 485 ac.; joining lines of Richard Johnson, Thomas Livesay,
formerly David Bell, Hugh McCormick, Elisha Poor and Jordan Harris,
vacant lands; Thomas Matthew's road and north fork David's Creek shown.

John Pankey; 13 ac.; June 24, 1801; adjoining Boatwright, Edward Patteson;
shows a road.

## Page 134

Colo. John Cabell; 127 ac.; joining lines of John Pankey, John Bagby, and
Colo. John Cabell; June 23, 1801. Note: 9 acres of Hugh McCormick 133
acres is survd to Cabell's tract by transfer from McCormick to Cabell
July 27, 1801. Note: 69 acres of land taken from Saml McCormick's 180
acres by transfer from Hugh McCormick to Sam ---- limiting him to 111
acres only and the works delivered for this quantity to John Cabell to
wit 205 acres; no dates.

Samuel McCormick; 180 acres - 69 acres = 111 acres; joining lines of John
Pankey, David Bell, Hugh McCormick and new lines just run for Colo
John Cabell; surveyed June 23, 1801. Note: July 27, 1801 this day
these works is granted to Saml McCormick for 111 acres by transfer from
Hugh McCormick.

Colo. John Cabell; 245 ac.; on July 20, 1801 by virtue of his location on a
land Office exchange warrt for 635 acres joining Absolum Thornhill; on
Howls Spring Branch; north fork David's Creek; John Stevens; Alteration
to Davids D---- September 14, 1801.

## Page 135

Absolum Thornhill; 61 ac.; joining John Stephens, Jordan Harris's and

Elisha Poor; August 4, 1800.

Robert Smith; 700 ac.; on waters Appomattox River and Fishpond Creek joining lines of Joseph Watkins, Samuel Hall, David Parrish, Davenport Woodson, and Robert Smith for the whom the survey was made June 10, 1801.

Robert Smith; 29 ac.; June 10, 1801; joining lines of Woodson and Joseph Watkins and his own; each side Fishpond Creek surveyed by virtue of Charles Maxey's warrt.

## Page 136

John Fergeson; 19 ac.; joining line of John Dolan, David Bell, John Pankey, and John Fergeson; March 6, 1801.

George Kelley; 15 ac.; joining lines of John Hardiman, John Gilliam, Richd Gilliam and George Kelley; March 13, 1801; this survey of 15 acres is made by Henry Rawlins exchange warrt for 389 acres.

Nathaniel Maxey; 96 ac.; June 19, 1801. joining John and James Walker.

John Childress; 100 ac.; joining lines of John Walker, Nathaniel Maxey, John Routen on waters of Hatchers branch of Holladay River; June 19, 1801.

## Page 137

Thomas Patteson; 144 ac.; December 29, 1801; each side of Ripley's Creek joining lines of Charles Patteson, Dudley Street, Reuben Puryear and Thomas Patteson.

Thomas Patteson; 246 ac.; December 29, 1801; each side Ripley's Creek joining lines of Reuben Puryear, David Pryor, Josiah Hatcher, John Patteson, and Thomas Patteson for whom the survey was made.

John West; 125 ac.; October 23, 1801; lying each side head of Briants Creek and on Glovers Road joining lines of Francis Harris and William Gipson.

## Page 138

Joseph Woldridge; 4 ac.; October 27, 1801; each side north fork Holloday River joining lines of the land that James Walker sold to David McCormick and which the said David sold to Joseph Woldridge and Thomas McCormick's lines.

Maj. Charles Yancey; 200 ac.; each side Bairds Road joining lines of Richd Gilliam, William Patteson, David McCormick and John Webb; October 16, 1801.

Griffin Garland; 1000 ac.; October --, 1801; on the ridge between the waters Slate River and Willis's each side of Murpheys road joining lines of James Wilson, David Warriner, and Loyd.

Page 139

Gresham Lee; 100 ac.; each side Wolf Creek of Appomattox River joining
   lines of Jesse Chandler, John Sears, the widow Jennings, Samuel
   Jennings and Gresham Lee on December 2, 1801.

Robert Smith; 30 ac.; joining lines of Samuel Hall and Robert Smith;
   December 4, 1801.

Samuel Watkins; 110 ac.; each side Burnetts Road joining lines Benjm
   Harrison, John Woodson, Joseph Watkins, Richard Peak; surveyed
   December 3, 1801. Note: March 15, 1803 this day Colo. Joel Watkins
   has located this tract of 110 acres of land and taken out works for
   the same.

Samuel Watkins; 32 ac.; on Appomattox River joining lines of Richard
   Peak, Joel Watkins, Samuel Watkins; December 3, 1801; Note: on
   March 15, 1803 this day Colo. Joel Watkins has located this tract
   of 32 acres of land and taken out works for the same.

Page 140

Willis Wills; 67 ac.; each side Bairds Road and joining lines of Hudson
   Morris, Dudley Brooks, Scayner (?) Scott, William Patteson, and
   John Morain; December 11, 1801.

Willis Wills; 150 ac.; December 12, 1801; joining lines of Josias Chambers,
   Wilson C. Nichols and each side of road leading from Warminster to
   New Canton and including the forks of the roads.

Peter Patteson; 89½ ac.; joining lines of Robert Smith, Richard Gilliam,
   and John Morain; October 4, 1801.

William Patteson; 230 3/4 ac.; each side of Bairds Road and joining line
   of Peter Patteson, John Morain, Saymer (?) Scott and Richard Gilliam ,
   October 4, 1801.

Page 141

Doctr David R. Patteson; 100 ac.; October 15, 1801; joining lines of Charles
   Yancey, Richd Gilliam, John Miller and John Webb.

James Gilliam; 100 ac.; October 15, 1801; joining Mr. John Miller, Taylor
   and Harrison, and John Webb.

Saml Coleman; 25 ac.; each side Bent Creek joining lines of Zachariah
   Griffiths, Robert Coleman and Saml Coleman; January 19, 1802; shows
   Thornhill's line.

Absolum Thornhill; 19 ac.; joining lines of Zachariah Griffiths, William
   Wright and Robert Coleman; January 19, 1802.

Samuel Coleman; 10 ac.; joining lines of Benja. Hardwick, Harden Woodroff, and Samuel Coleman; January 22, 1802.

Page 142

John Ferguson; 64 ac.; joining lines of Mr. Dougald Ferguson, James Burnett and John Ferguson; January 23, 1802; a road shown.

Edward L. Page and Thomas Brothers; 34 ac.; February 4, 1802; each side David's Creek joining lines of Horseley and Freeland, Mace Freeland, and Joseph C. Megginson.

Mace Freeland; 13 ac.; each side of a pair of road paths joining lines of Taliferro and Chick(?) and Mace Freeland; February 3, 1803.

Edward Curd; 50 ac.; each side Long Branch and joining Saunders, Morrow, Eavins; July 29, 1800.

John and William Curd; 11½ ac.; joining lines of M. Hobson, the widow Lumkin, and William Curd; July 29, 1800.

Page 143

William Staples; 150 ac.; June 3, 1802; on waters Stonewall Creek joining lines of Archibald Bolling, Nathl Hood, the Campbell line and William Staples for whom the survey was made.

Samuel Smith; 300 ac.; March 18, 1802; on each side middle fork Slate River joining lines of William McFaddin and John Briant.

Nathanial Garrett; 48 ac.; September 9, 1800; joining lines of Joshua Nicholas, Abner Seay, Joseph Roper and Nathanial Garrett.

Page 144

Nathaniel Williams; 50 ac.; May 22, 1802; joining lines of John Pittman, James Wilson, Griffin Garland, John Epperson and Benjamin Loyd.

Leonard Ballowe; 6½ ac.; June 4, 1802; including Slate River 38 poles and joining Henry Jackson, Joseph Cunningham and land formerly patented to Henry Hamilton and George H. Allen; on Rocky Creek.

Finch Scruggs; 68 3/4 ac.; joining lines of Vallantine Scruggs, Allen Scruggs, George H. Allen (Inft) and the legatees of Stephen Perrow decd; August 5, 1802.

John Miller; 183 ac.; August 11, 1802; joining lines Andrew Flowers, John Tuggles, Robert Rodgers, and lines of Capt John Miller for whom the survey was made.

Page 145

John Miller; 87 ac.; September 15, 1802; joining lines of Rhoda McLoyd,

Nicholas old line. Resurveyed with David Kyles warrt and works issued July 30, 1803 and the survey bears date accordingly.

John Miller; 40 ac.; September 15, 1802; joining lines of Rhoda McLoyd, and on east end of Willis's Mountain; this 40 acres reentered with David Kyle's warrant.

Henry Woldridge; 133 ac.; including the Round Mountain joining lines of Elizabeth Childress, Hooper, Curd, and Joshua Nicholas's old lines. September 24, 1802.

John Pankey and Thomas Patteson; 230 ac.; September 24, 1802; including Willis's Mountain joining lines of Joshua Nicholas old tract, Henry Woldridge, and the widow Childress.

Page 146

John Baskerville; 184 ac.; joining lines of Thomas Ellyson and Christian's order of Council; May 31, 1802.

Thomas Ellyson; 10 ac.; May 31, 1802; near the waters of Wreck Island Creek joining lines of Christian's order of council, John Baskerville, and Thomas Ellyson.

John Baskerville; 54 ac.; November 13, 1802; joining lines of Mace Freeland, Mace Pendleton, and George Allen and William Badberry.

William C. Murrey; 169 ac.; December 4, 1802; south side and adjoining Fluvanna River joining lines of Randolph Jefferson and Harden Perkins.

William Watson; 10 ac.; November 6, 1802; each side of the road leading from Buckingham Courthouse to town of Warren in Albemarle and joining lines of Josiah Hatcher, David Pryor and John Patteson.

Page 147

Peter H. Ware; 1000 ac.; September 9, 1802; joining lines of Samuel Anderson, Henry Bell and lines of Archibald Carey decd; on Hatcher's Creek; joining Henry Carey's 3942 acres.

Peter H. Ware; 160 ac.; September 10, 1802; formerly Jno Gresham now Samuel and George Anderson, surveyed for the benefit of Peter H. Ware and to establish the said Ware beginning.

Josias Jones; 40 ac.; joining lines of Edward Jones, Jesse Smith (infant) and his own lines; April 25, 1803.

Joseph Horsley; 10 ac.; joining lines John Burks, Booth and Staples, and his own lines; May 14, 1803.

Page 148

James Freeland and David Kyle; 126 ac.; February 23, 1803; joining lines of Joseph C. Megginson, David Kyle and Spears.

John Flowers; 93 ac.; joining south side Bairds Road joining lines of Cary
Harrison decd, Hall and Gallohorn and Falweil; May 9, 1803.

Jacob Maxey; 7 ac.; July 38, 1803; joining lines of Benjm More, William
Spencer, and Noah Flood.

James Gilliam; 100 ac.; joining lines Alexander Faubush (?), John Webb,
Joseph Woldridge, and Thomas McCormick; December 22, 1802.

## Page 149

William Allen; 18 ac.; August 16, 1803; lines of Capt Benjm Harriss, Samuel
Jordan decd, George H. Allen (inft) and Nunnally.

Absolum Thornhill; 42 ac.; October 31, 1803; on a branch of David's Creek
joining lines of land Mr. Harriss sold to Benjamin More.

Irving, Charles decd; 22 ac.; no date; on each side Ballowes Creek joining
lines of legatees of Charles Irving vizt: Janne Rose, Charles Irving,
Robert Irving, Mildred Irving, and Paulus A. Irving.

Ellyson Harvie; 200 ac.; February 9, 1804; each side of the county line
joining the lines of Morriss, Cary Harrison and the lines of Ellyson
Harvie himself.

Jones Phipps; 40 ac.; March 16, 1804; joining lines of John Wright, William
Gowing, and William Chick.

## Page 150

Robert M. Corder; 14 ac.; joining lines of David Parish, Robert Smith and
Warner Williams; April 12, 1804.

Robert M. Corker; 55 ac.; joining lines of David Parrish and Robert Smith;
April 12, 1804.

John Turner; 200 ac.; joining lines of Little Berry Moon, John Chambers,
James Staton and John Turner; May 19, 1804.

Sherwood McCormick; 10 ac.; each side Murphey's Road joining lines of Samuel
McCormick, Richard Gilliam, Greens, and Moses Flood; surveyed for
Sherwood McCormick who sold it to Samuel McCormick; November 23, 1803.

Thomas Pattison; 56 ac.; joining lines of Mr. James Staton, John Anderson,
and Richard West; November 23, 1803; Note: This survey is made for
Bennet Maxey and Mary B. Anderson March 23, 1826, signed John Patteson.

## Page 151

David Pryor; 45 ac.; assigned to L. Pryor and by him to Thomas East; joining
lines of Thomas Anderson; September 1803.

George Perkins; 310 ac.; on waters of Fish Pond Creek a branch of Appomattox
River joining lines of Warner Williams, Samuel Hall, George Chandler,

Hall and Gallohorn, Peter Patteson and old lines the proprietors name unknown; May 30, 1804.

William Newton; 7 ac.; August 10, 1804; joining lines of the legatees of John Sanders and south side and joining Willis's River.

Robert Nicholas; 3 ac.; December 5, 1804; joining lines of Charles Perrow, George Nicholas, and Robert Nicholas himself.

Charles A. Scott; 5 ac.; joining to Slate River and line of the land the said Charles A Scott bought of Mr. Robert Nicholas; November 22, 1804; 5 acres lying about 500 yards above his mill on Slate River joining to the lines formerly Nicholas.

Page 152

Capt. Peter Guerrant Jr.; 570 ac.; November 7, 1804; on waters of Hunts Creek joining lines of William Allen, Old Capt Peter Guerrants line of the tract he lives on, Charles Perrow, 14 poles only on Mr. George Nicholas, and the land commonly known and called the furnace lands surveyed for Peter Guerrant Jr. Note: This line was run in making Peter Guerrant's survey of 500 ac. on February 21, 1806 and ---80 acres.

John Patteson; 60 ac.; November 15, 1804; joining lines the legatees of Benjamin Tindal decd and Robert Jones; surveyed for John Patteson principal surveyor.

Page 153

Legatees of Thomas Anderson; 41 ac.; April 4, 1805; lower side of Rock Island Creek joining lines of Mr. Price Perkins, and legatees of Thomas Anderson decd; surveyed for Nathl Anderson, Robert Rives, and John Harriss as executors of Thomas Anderson decd. Warrant and works issued to Capt. Nathl Anderson April 9, 1805.

Capt. Daniel Bagby; 420 ac.; joining lines George Nicholas, Peter Guerrants new survey and the furnace tract each side of the road leading from Hamilton's ford to New Canton and the old tract road. December 18, 1804. On a branch of Hunts Creek.

Capt. Daniel Bagby; 2 ac.; joining lines Robert Smith, Thomas Baber and Robert Hill; December 20, 1804.

Page 154

William Watson; May 20, 1805; 60 ac.; joining legatees of Benjamin Tindal decd and Robert Jones.

Richard Hardiman; March 23, 1805; 12 ac.; joining lines of John Jones, Capt. Charles Moseley and John Hardiman; near Pickshin Road.

Isaac Sallee; May 25, 1805; 9 ac.; joining lines of Holeman's legatees and ?.

George Perkins; September 2, 1805; 80 ac.; joining lines of John Brothers, Nortly Gordan's old lines, Joseph Clarks, John Baskerville and Thomas

Ellyson.

Richard Cottrell; August 23, 1805; 22 ac.; joining lines Kidd and his own lines.

## Page 155

William Allen; August 21, 1805; 120 ac.; joining lines of Thomas Baber and the tract commonly called the furnace tract; shows Smith's and B----'s corner.

William Allen; August 21, 1805; 5 ac.; each side Bear Garden Creek and joining lines of Thomas Beaber and James Moss; shows low ground of Bear Garden Creek and creek itself.

Capt. Dan'l Bagby; August 22, 1805; 41 ac.; joining lines of Mr. George Nicholas, the land commonly called the Furnace Land, Capt. Dan'l Bagby's own lines and new lines.

Peter Guerrant Jr.; August 20, 1805; 34 ac.; joining John Guerrant, Stephen Guerrant, and Walton and adjoining to the south side of Slate River.

John J. Brown; April 19, 1805; 6 ac.; joining lines of Mr. Allen, William Jones, Ammonett and Capt. Thomas J. Price.

## Page 156

Peter Guerrant Jr.; 420 ac.; August 19, 1805; joining lines of Mr. Nicholas, the furnace lands and Peter Guerrant Jr; branch of Hunt's Creek, Tract Road and another road shown; new lines.

Rolin West; May 18, 1805; 497½ ac.; on waters Rock Island Creek joining lines of John Watkins, Rays, James Staton, John Anderson, Lenaius (also spelled Laeneaus) Bolling and Isham Milton.

William Spencer; January 25, 1806; 200 ac.; joining lines of John Hardiman, Peter Dupeay, and William Spencer; near Pond Creek.

## Page 157

Capt. Benjamin More (? - blurred); February --, 1806; 13 ac.; by virtue of his location on Exchange Land Office Treasury Warrant No. 1472 and dated August 17, 1803 and bounded by Livesey, own lines and an unnamed branch.

Peter North; October 19, 1805; 7 3/4 ac.; joining lines of Nicholas Turner, Thomas Ellyson, and John Birks; surveyed by John Harris for John Patteson, Surveyor BC.

Jas. Freeland; December 23, 1805; 41 ac.; waters David's Creek joining lines of David Kyle, Joseph (C) Meginson and Mace Freeland. This is a long, narrow parcel.

John Wright; February 6, 1806; 40 ac.; joining William Garvin(g), William Chick, James Wright and John Wright.

## Page 158

William Patteson; April 6, 1806; 41 ac.; waters Fish Pond Creek by virtue of his location on land office treasury warrant No. ----(blank) and bounded by Robert M. Corker, George Chandler, John Beasleys old line, Cary Harrison dec'd; crossing two branches.

Peter Guerrant; February 22, 1806; 500 ac.; joining lines of the furnace tract of land, George Nicholas, and Charles Perrow on waters of Hunts Creek showing old tract road and road "from Hamilton's ford to N. Carter."

Rolfe Eldridge; April 4, 1806; 200 ac.; each side Turpin's Creek joining James Agee, Rolfe Eldridge Sen., new lines and land "supposed to be vacant."

## Page 159

Joseph Evans; April 23, 1806; 74 ac.; joining lines of Mr. Dennis Murphey, Boaz Ford, James Agee, Rolfe Eldridge and Joseph Evans.

Joseph Eavans (sic); 150 ac.; April 23, 1806; joining lines of Mr. Rolfe Eldridge Sr., James Agee, and Mr. Rolfe Eldridge Jr.

William Watson; March 15, 1806; 40 ac.; joining lines of the Widow (crossed out) Rhoda McLoyd and on the east end Willisses Mountain.

## Page 160

Armistead Garnett; October 1, 1806; 32 ac.; joining lines John Childress, William Hooper and Nathanield Garnett and "new lines lately run by John Woodson and said to be Nath'l Garnetts."

Legatees of William Coffee dec'd; in Buckingham and Prince Edward; 191 ac.; on both side Appomattox River; legatees - Pleasant Coffee and Joshua Coffee division by order of Court and by direction of commissioners and joining lines of Thomas Trent, the Commonwealth's land, John Land and John Sears. Large, detailed survey. October 8, 1806. Shows river and branches; Pleasant Coffee got 138 ac., Joshua Coffee got 95 ac. Also shows Megruder's land.

## Page 161

Samuel McCormick; 25 ac.; 28 November 1806; joining lines of John Cabell, Benjm Maxey and Benjm More.

Joseph Walling; 400 ac.; October 17, 1806; waters Hunts Creek, each side of the road leading from Hamilton's ford on Slate River to New Canton and each side of the Old Tract road leading from Buckingham Court House to New Canton and joining lines of Mr. George Nicholas, Peter Guerrant,

and lines of land commonly called and known by the Buckingham furnace
lands; surveyed by Joseph Walling at and by the direction of William
Hansford by John Harris Jr. asst for John Patteson surv Buckingham Co.

William Bigbie; November 22, 1806; 400 ac.; joining Bowman, George E.
Diuguid, Major Flood, Peter Patteson, Jas. Patteson; on Bridle or
Bent Creek.

## Page 162

Rezin Porter; March 31, 1806; 300 ac.; waters Fishpond Creek and joining lines
of Samuel Hall, Warner Williams, David (P) Cockes, and his own lines,
Cary Harrison dec'd.

Phil. Duval; April 3, 1806; 35 ac.; waters Wreck Island Creek joining lines
of James Hundley's survey, John Christian decd and his own survey.

Robert Moseley; February 14, 1807; 12 ac.; waters Slate River joining lines
of Charles Moseley, Thomas Jones and Moses Spencer.

## Page 163

George H. Allen; 15 ac.; December 10, 1807; on north side of and joining
Slate River; joining Hill, Winfrey.

William Steger; 2½ ac.; December 10, 1807; joining Bransford; Sam Steger,
Jos Cunningham, each side Old Woman's alias Rocky Creek.

Capt. William Allen's; survey and division agreeable to the last will and
testament of Capt. William Allen; **William Allen** 610 ac.; Elizabeth
Allen 400 ac., on Church Road; Philip and John Allen 240 ac.; on Hunts'
Creek; William Allen 34 ac.; joining Capt William Allen; Hardwick
Branch; William Allen's 214 ac. survey; Peter Guerrants Gold Mine
Tract; Jacob Agee formerly Terry Galloways now Peter Guerrants.

## Page 164

This is one long, narrow survey for Peter Guerrant; November 18, 1807;
490 ac.; on and near waters Hunts Creek and joining lines of William
Allen, Peter Guerrant Senr, Charles Perrow; his own **survey** of 500 ac.
and a tract generally known and called the furnace tract of land;
Mill Branch shown.

## Page 165

Capt John Couch division; "land late the property of Capt John Couch; 1324
ac.; on south bank and adjoining the Fluvanna River; November 2, 1813;
"surveyed and divided by virtue of a decree from the Honble High Court
of Chancery for the Richmond District; Lot No. 1 containing 774 ac.
and lot No. 2 containing 550 ac. the widow's dower being a part of each
lot and included within the red marked lines, the dotted lines from A
to B and due south 320 poles as laid down in the general survey,
constitutes the dividing line between No. 1 and No. 2; joining lines

of Maj. David Patteson, Capt Jno Staples, Chls Staton, Capt John
Couch, Capt Samuel Shelton, Thomas J. Anderson, John ----(?; illegible); shows Warren Road; a meeting house on Warren Road; Thos.
Tindall's home in lot 2; 108 ac. as Mrs. Couch's dower and Mrs.
Couch's house; Samuel Shelton's mills at ---- Creek and Fluvanna
River. David Patteson's lines are directly south of this survey.

Page 166

Survey and division of property of Capt. William Allen dec'd; containing
1336 ac; Lot No. 1 of 433 ac. laid off for Richard Cobbs and Elizth
C. Cobb's his wife; and Lot No. 2 including the dwelling house of 903
ac. was reserved for Phillip and John Allen; Lot No. 3 between the
Church Road and the original tract is a bequest of 240 ac. of land
from old Capt William Allen dec'd to Phillip and John Allen; December 7,
1807; joining lines of Thomas Bransford, Stephen Guerrant, William Allen
(son of George); Hardwick's Branch, Ford's line, John Allen, Arthr
Sherrons(?); an uncertain line; Sanders; Rene Chastain; Deep Bottom
Creek; an old mill; a dwelling house.

Page 167

George Nicholas; June 2, 1808; 16 ac.; joining lines of Daniel Bagby, the
furnace tract and his own lines.

Stephen Martin; 8 ac.; February 3, 1809; each side Court House Road joining
lines of Matthew Branch, Rolfe Eldridge Jr. and Majr Benjm Moseley decd.

Edward Lewis; 10 ac.; October 26, 1808; on each side booring branch and
joining lines James Patteson, Littlebury Hughes and John (M) Walker.

Randolph Harrison; October 15, 1808; 2½ ac.; joining lines of David Ross
and his own lines.

Page 168

Large survey for Samuel P. Christian Lot No. 2, 432 ac shows dwelling house;
Capt Chas Philps Lot No. 1 408 ac.; shows another dwelling house; on
Stillhouse branch, Bent Creek Road; no other notes, no date, no
neighbors. Appears to be a division; shows an unnamed creek and road.

Page 169

Capt Daniel Bagby; 420 ac.; December 11, 1807; each side the road leading
from Hamilton's ford on Slate River to New Canton also each side of
the Old Tract Road and adjoining lines of George Nicholas, Peter
Guerrants ----, the land generally called and known by the furnace
lands; a road shown.

Francis Walthal 17 ac.; March 24, 1808; joining lines Benjm Morriss and
Nathl Morriss; "a bunch of bushes in an old field" a marker.

Austin Bryant; 25 ac.; May 31, 1808; joining lines of John Bryant, Jas

Cunningham, John Falwell and Tapscotts'.

## Page 170

Anthony Bryant; 10 ac.; 31 May 1808; joining lines of Thomas Cobbs and his own lines.

John Dolan; November 1, 1808; 32 ac.; on a branch of Jon(es)(?) Mill Creek and joining lines of Claibourn Maxey, John Wright and J. Dolan.

Daniel Guerrant; 145 ac.; 2 June 1808; adjoining the Fluvanna or James River just above the town of New Canton and joining lines of George Nicholas, the furnace tract, the widow Blanks.

## Page 171

Mr. Thomas Bransford; 35 ac.; December 21, 1809; joining lines of Noah Agee and Rene Chastain.

Thomas Bransford; 130 ac.; December 21, 1809; joining lines of Noah Agee, Rane Chastain and Allen's lines.

Danl Guerrant; 17 ac.; 31 January 1810; on each side of the New Canton Road joining lines of the furnace and the land of George Nicholas sold to Alex Garrott.

Rueben Amonet; 18 ac.; 17 January (1810?); joining lines of Thomas J. Price, George Allen and his own lines.

## Page 172

Gabriel Wright's dec'd legatees; February 1809; 288 ac.; surveyed by Nelson Patteson asst surv. to J. Patteson Surveyor of Buckingham. Shows widow's dower of 92 ac .; other lots but no names of legatees Joining lines of Clay, William Gill, D. Woodall, Obadiah Harris, Edmund Winston.

A survey of 195 2/3 ac. in 1809; no names given; 1/3 part taken as a dower.

## Page 173

Reubin Amonett; 124 ac.; February 22, 1810; joining William Amonett, James Snody, George Allen.

Boaz Ford; 105 ac.; February 23, 1810; north side Turpin's Creek; joining James Flowers, Thomas Thomas, and his own lines.

John Jamison's dec'd legatees; February 22, 1810; 157 ac.; waters Little Buffalo Creek and joining lines of Ford's legatees, Thomas Christian, Carter Adcock, Talley and Peter May. Shows lots for widow Jamison,(50 ac.) Nancy Jameson (33½ ac.), Daniel Jamison (37½ ac.) and John Harris (36 ac.).

Thomas May; 160 ac.; 22 February 1810; on Allen's Quarter Road joining Edward Maxey, Thomas Bondurant and John Chambers.

### Page 174

Survey of a tract divided by Anthony Dibrell, John Gary and John Pattison "who was mutually chosed by Miles Gipson and Jacob L. Abrahams and admitted to record." February 23, 1810; 406 ac.; each side Walton's fork; joining Miles Gibson (203 ac.) Jacob L. Abraham (203 ac.) and Anthony Dibrell; also joining Benj. Radford's line, Major Oakes, and James Terry.

Legatees of Thos. Cobbs dec'd; February 13, 1810; 630 ac.; each side of two forks Rock Island Creek belonging to legatees of Thomas Cobbs decd; joining Samuel Birks lines; Briant, Colo. Wilson, Cary Harrison, James Couch, and Thomas Carter; legatees not named.

### Page 175

William Kennon dec'd; 4533 ac.; entire survey barely fits on page -- some surrounding information cut off; plat of land claimed by heirs of William Kennon dec'd on waters of Wreck Island Creek, Bent Creek and a part thereof joining James River; joining lines of John Christian dec'd, Richd North, Peter North, John Birks, T--- Ellyson, John Baskerville, George Perkins, Solomon Williams, William Chick, Mace Freeland, Mace Pendleton, George Allen and John Walker. Resurveyed August 31, 1809 agreeable to an order of the (High) Court of Chancery, holden at the Capitol in Richmond the 9th day of February 1809 at and by the ------ William Chick, ageant (sic) for the heirs of William Kennon dec'd. Shows Wreck Island in James and Wreck Island Creek.

### Page 176

William Mathews; 170 3/4 ac.; on both sides Randolph's Creek and joining lines of John Woodson, James Meredith, William Mathews and William I Berryman; February 28, 1810; part of survey is cut off; appears to be a division

Robin Burton dec'd; 513 ac.; on south side James River divided among the legatees of Robin Burton dec'd and adjoining lines of Daniel Bagby, John Adams, Peter Guerrant and other (no other names listed though); March 6,7,8, 9, 1810; joining John Guerrant, and Hansford; Legatees listed: John Ballowe (49½ ac), Jane Burton (44 ac), Douglass Burton (49½ ac), Patsy Burton (? ac), Micajah Burton (49½ ac), Jacob Burton (49½ ac), Elizabeth Burton (167 ac), Nathaniel Burton (49 ac).

### Page 177

Legatees of Capt. John Sanders; 700 ac.; connected plat and dividend; both sides Willises Creek and waters thereof adjoining lines of Claiborne West, James Sanders, William Johns, and Capt William Jones; divisions shown without names; no date.

A connected plat a part of which constitutes the line in controversy between Nathaniel Garrett on one side and Elizabeth Hooper and ----

William Hooper the other side; Nathaniel Garrett is in possession
and claims Lot No. 1 containing 400 ac. by Samuel Ridgways patent
baring date March 15, 1744 and ----Hooper and her son William Hooper
is in possession of and claims Lot 2 of 395 ac. under William Fry's
Patent baring date 15 December 1749. On Tongue Quarter Creek.
Buckingham Court January 1808 a jury viewed the area and ordered
adjustments. Jury (most names cut off): David Warner, Nathaniel
Morris, William Gibson (?), Edmond ----, Joseph ----, rest illegible.

## Page 178

George Tabscott; 156 3/4 ac.; on both sides Rock Island Creek and joining
lines of R. Slaton, Burgess, Darby Bondurant and Tabscott. May 23, 1810.

John Harris; 9½ ac.; joining lines of Lydia Diuguid, and Thomas Walton;
June 8, 1812.

Survey of 13 ac.; joining lines of Joseph Burks, George Christian, Shadrah
Smith, Anthony North, Benjamin Bailey; June 8, 1810.

Saymer Scott; 337 ac.; joining lines of John Childress, Nathaniel Garrett;
John Sanders, Benjamin Hooper, and Spencer Watkins, June 15, 1810.

William Slaton; 150 ac.; 19 June 1810; joining lines of John Staples,
James Slaton, Jr., Charles Slaton, Capt John Couch, James Couch,
William Slaton's own lines; on Howard's Road and Warren Road; a
branch shown.

## Page 179

Survey of 1293 ac.; adjoining Holloday River and waters Fish Pond; 1159 ac.
being made in one survey and 93 in one survey and 41 in one survey as
per the annexed plat survd the 20th and 21st July 1810; works dated
21st and under and virtue of Cary Harrison's entries upon Land Office
Treasury warrant of 2000 ac.; Joining Robert M. Corker, Rezin Porter,
William Brown, Joseph Brown, Alexr Faubush, Thomas McCormack, Fowle,
Sam'l Smith, Cary Harrison dec'd, Falwell's lines.

## Page 180

Survey of 360 ac.; north side Muddy Creek and joining lines of Robert Craigg,
Mrs. Winiford and Maxys, 250 ac of which was sold by Bernard Nunnally
to Thomas E. Pleasants and laid off of the above tract as laid down
September 12, 1810.

Stephen Sanders and Elijah H. Hendrick; 340 ac.; south side Willises River
adjoining lines of Edward Curd, Benjamin Morris and Phill Hodnell;
August 17, 1810.

Survey of 2 ac.; including Buckingham Court House and Jail; laid off agreeable
to an order of court of Buckingham for the benefit of the public by the
commissioners the 22nd day of September 1810. Shows Court House and
jail locations.

Page 181

Survey of 230 ac.; east side of a road leading from Buckingham Court House to Warren and adjoining lines of James Slaton Jr., James Slaton Sr., Capt J. Staples, Major David Patteson, and Capt John Couch. Surveyed for Iverson Warner on August 3, 1810.

John Gannoway; 338 ac.; 18 August 1810; north side Willis' River and adjoining lines of Lewis Wilkinson, John Morrow, William Evans, James Hubbard, David and Cary Stinson.

George Tapscott; 6ac.; 31 August 1810; adjoining lines of Darby Bondurant and George Tapscott and Mrs. Tapscott.

James Slaton; 194 ac.; 11 September 18(10)(?); joining lines of James Slaton Jr., Jesse Couch and Samuel Berks. Surveyed for Doctr David R. ----- attorney in fact for Simon Hudson by virtue of two warrants each for 100 ac. and sold by him to James Slaton Jr.

Page 182

Robert Anderson; 116 ac.; both sides Walton's fork and adjoining lines of Abraham Neighbors, Nelson Shelton, Miller, and Robert Anderson; October 1, 1810.

Price Perkins; Lot No. 2 = 515 ac. shows dwelling house; on waters of Walton's Fork; Mrs. Blakey's dower Lot No. 1 = 515 ac.; shows barn and dwelling house; Taylor's Creek; joining lines of David Patteson, Wilson C. Nicholas, Thomas Davis, Anthony Dibrell, David Patteson (again) and Price Perkins. Shows a division.

Survey of 50 ac.; north side Willis' River joining lines of Edward and John Sanders; November 15, 1810; for whom?

Page 183

Samuel P. Christian; 28 ac.; joining lines of Thomas Logwood, Charles Staples, Jno Walker and his own lines; March 4, 1811.

Samuel P. Christian; 6½ ac.; joining lines of Charles Statham (?), Charles Staples and Samuel P. Christian; March 4, 1811.

Jno. M. Walker; 25 ac.; February 4, 1811; joining lines of Samuel P. Christian and his own lines.

Survey and division of land late the property of Robert Moore dec'd and containing 488 ac. lying on waters David's Creek; division by order of Powhatan Court dated 16 January 1811 which order had reference to another order of 19 December 1810. Devisees: Thomas Moore (lot 3, 106 ac), William Moore (lot 2, 140 ac), Jno Moore (lot 1, ?ac), lot 4 102 ac (no name attached). On branch of David's Creek; road from

Buckihgham Court House; Bent Creek; joining lines of Colo Jno Cabell, Moores, Henneseys, Jno Baky, Jno Staples.

## Page 184

Map of the town of New Canton, surveyed at the order of the trustees by John Patteson, Surveyor Buckingham County on 20 day of March 1811. Shows town lots and streets but not owners.

## Page 185

Survey of 492 ac.; on head branches of Whispering Creek surveyed for Reubin Ammonett; April 26, 1811; joining new lines, Joseph Agee, Hezekiah Lipscomb, Page, Anderson Lipscomb 211½ ac., Jessee Jefferies 280½ ac.; (apparently a division).

Survey of 98 ac.; Stephen Guerrant; on waters Greens Creek made September 19, 1811; joining Thomas Bransford, Noah Agee and Allen.

## Page 186

Survey made April 1, 1811 at request of William Chick agent for heirs of William Kennon dec'd and persuant to an order from Superior Court of Cancery (sic) for Richmond Districk (sic) "I have surveyed the above track of 4742 ac.; each side Wreck Island Creek, joining Fluvvanna River which was begun on 1 April 1811 and finished the same week by patent bearing date 15 May 1790 in name of Jerman Baker and James Belchers surviving trustees of William Kennon dec'd joining George Allen, John Walker, John Christian; land formerly Thomas Matthews, Peter North, John Birks, Thomas Ellyson, John Baskerville, Solomon Williams, William Chick; shows Broad Branch, Wreck Island Creek, and Wreck Island.

## Page 187

Jarrot Patteson; 22 ac.; on waters David's Creek belonging to Jarrot Patteson; joining lines of Edward Patteson. James Agee, Hardin Woodroof and William Flood; December 4, 1812; December 26, 1818: This day this plat and certif. is granted to William Stephens for his 22 acres of land by his location.

Benajah Brown; August 6, 1812; 150 ac.; on Hatcher's Creek; joining lines of George Eldridge, John J. Brown dec'd, Henry Grizzles, Nathan Ayres (formerly Paus?)(alias Ayres) and a new line said to be Fishers and Carrs line surveyed by virtue of a deed from the marshal of this district to John J. Brown dec'd and of Record in the County Court of Buckingham.

Peter North; 4½ ac.; waters Wreck Island Creek; joining lines of Robert Rodgers and John Miller dec'd; July 20, 1812.

## Page 188

Jas Patteson; 36 ac.; waters Wreck Island Creek and joining lines of William Bigbie, Thomas Chancellor, Abraham Nowlin, and John and James Patteson. June 5, 1812.

Jas Patteson; 6 ac.; June 5, 1812; waters Wreck Island Creek joining John Patteson and Abraham Nowlin.

David Patteson; 27 ac.; joining lines of Thomas Tindal, Thomas Jefferson. Anderson and David Patteson; November 3, 1813.

## Page 189

Survey and division of 1012 ac.; late property of Mrs. Susannah Wilcox decd and divided by order of County Court of Buckingham amongst the distributees; date?. Lot No. 1 275 ac.; Lot No. 2 260 ac.; Lot No. 3 195 ac.; Lot No. 4 282 ac.; no names on lots; house shown; on north fork Buffalo Creek. Joining lines of James Wilson, Coupland, Wheeler, Anderson, Bell's legatees, William Gay, Strong, C. Wisdow(??)Wilson.

George Carson; 140 ac.; 10 May 1815; joining Joseph Watkins, Gresham Lee, Capt George Perkins, and his own lines.

## Page 190

Survey of 240 ac.; south side Hatcher's Creek for Samuel Anderson; October 20, 1815 by virtue of his land warrant for 250 acres dated October 2, 1815; joining the Belmont (?) tract of land; near Halfway Branch.

John Forbes; April 1818(?) 10 ac.; by virtue of his land warrant for 384 acres, No. 1816 and dated January 17, 1816 joining William Patteson, Smith's line, Jno Maurain, Hudson Morriss and Jno. Walker.

Jacob Maxey; 23 ac.; 1 November 1816; near Jones Mill Creek joining John Dolling and Jacob Maxey.

## Page 191

Stephen Routon; 13 3/4 ac.; virtue of his location on exchange land office Treasury Warrant of 384 acres dates January 17, 1806 and No. 1816; joining John Morris, John Routon decd, Thompsons Creek, Claiborn Harris.

John West; 6½ ac.; joining lines of Thomas Miller and his own lines. July 18, 1817.

## Page 192

By a decree from the Honorable the (Judge of the ) Superior Court of Chancery for Richmond District as will appear in the report annexed on next page (not there); Thomas Wilson No. 2, 75 ac.; Thomas Wilson No. 3, 181 ac.; Colo John Nicholas No. 4, 114 ac.; Doct Tell(?) Morris No. 1, 61 ac.; on Slate River and Hunts Creek (these are shown).

## Page 193

John M. Walker; 23 ac.; joining lines of John M Walker, William Moore, and Meshack Boaz; April 6, 1826.

John M. Walker; 14 ac.; April 6, 1826; joining lines of Meshack Boaz and his own lines.

Charles Hamner; 31 ac.; joining Wade Boatwright, Charles W. Hamner and John M. Walker. May 2, 1826.

David W. Glover; 207 ac.; 29 August 1826; 20 ac.; by virtue of his location on land office treasury warrant for 500 acres No. 9064 and dated 21 August 1826; joining Moseley's Rolling Road, Moseleys, Mrs. Walkers, Samuel Pattesons; shows a road.

## Page 194

Warner Williams; 44 ac.; joining lines of estate of Michael Jones dec'd Will's survey, William Andrews and William McKinney. November 16, 1827.

Leneous Bolling; September 28(?), 1830; 464 ac; by virtue of his location on two land office treasury warrants one for 400 acres No. 10264 and dated 25 April 1829 and other an exchange warrant of 86 acres No. 2515 and dated 3 April 1826 and joining James W. Winfrey, little George's Creek, Mrs. Nicholas, James or Fluvanna River.

John Henderson; 13 ac.; joining Charles Hamner and John Henderson; June 20, 1831; joining Mace --- Spencer near Wreck Island Creek.

## Page 195

Capt. George Booker; 1332 ac.; on waters of Holliday River joining lines of Alex. Forbes, Capt Joseph Wooldridge, Rebecca McCormick, Saml Smith dec'd, Baird's Road, Falwell, Feazley, Chandler, Rezin Porter, William Brown and Company, Joseph Brown decd; July 31, 1818.

## Page 196

William W. Wilbourn; 12 ac.; joining lines of Matt Cox and Danl Guerrant January 21, 1819.

Stephen Routon; December 15, 1819; by virtue of his location on Exchange land office Treasury Warrant of 360½ ac., No. 2276 dated 20 April 1818; joining Danl Moseley, Thomas Gary and his own.

Thomas T. Thornhill; 11 ac.; August 2, 1820; by virtue of his location on Land office Treasury Warrant of 100 ac. No. 6381 and dated October 17, 1818; joining David Kyle and William Thornhill.

John Gary; 6 ac.; joining lines of the land known and called by the Mulberry Grove Tract, late the property of Prettyman Merry and the lines of John Gary; April 14, 1821. Surveyed by Danl Guerrant; warrant of 250 acres dated October 2, 1815; warrant sent to Registers office with the survey.

Page 197

These plats were surveyed and divided by order of court in December 1812 between the Legatees of Edmond Glover decd. Plat number 1: Dry Creek and the River: Richard William 100 acres lot 8; Micajah Scruggs 100 acres lot 9; Benjamin Glover 50 acres lot 10; William Glover 50 acres lot 11; James Glover 95 acres lot 12; John Bristoe 20(?) acres lot 13. Plat number 2: George Glover ?acres lot 7; Patsy Glover 50 acres lot 6; Thomas Glover 45 acres lot 5; Lucy Glover 50 acres lot 44; Judith Glover 50 acres lot 3; Edmond Glover 50 acres lot 2; Wilson Brooks 52 acres lot 1.

Jno Bristow; 316 ac.; south side Glover's Road being part of the division of the above estate and constituting lot 13 drawn by Jno Bristow December 15, 1813.

George Carson; 350 ac.; waters of Fish Pond Creek a branch of Appomattox River and joining lines of Gresham Lee, Capt George Perkins and Joseph Watkins; May 14, 1814.

Page 198

George Carson and George Billups; 140 ac.; joining lines of George Perkins, Gresham Lee, and George Carsons; May 14, 1814.

Survey of 1000 ac. and division on waters of Slate River by direction of Major Charles Yancey, Rolfe Eldridge and Samuel Jones commissioners who acted under decree of high Court of Chancery Richmond District land lately held by Robt Kincaid; joining Edmond Glover legatees, Charles Jones, new lines joining Alexander Trent, and Thomas May's shows Kincaid's old dwelling house; Glover's Creek; a wheat mill; Briant's Creek.

Page 199

Elisha Maxey; 20 December 1820; 3 ac.; by warrant of 100 acres No. 4907 joining Edward Maxey, William Maxey, Elisha Maxey.

Andrew White; April 5, 1822; 15½ ac.; by warrant of 100 acres No. 6894 dated May 1, 1820; joining William Dillon, Robert Rives, Rives McLane and Co.; shaped like a bow tie

Edward Chambers; 3 ac.; joining lines of Robert Anderson and Edward Chambers; April 26, 1823.

William D. Jones; 2 ac.; joining lines of Capt Samuel Branch and William D. Jones; December 16 (?), 1823.

Page 200

Colo John Horsley; August 3, 1825; 40 ac.; by virtue of his location on Land Office Treasury Warrant of 100 acres No. 6927 dated July 20, 1820; joining Rives, Murphy and White and Horsley's own lines.

Lenues Bolling; 14 ac.; joining lines of Mrs. Martha Nicholas and L. Bolling; November 23, 1825.

Bennet Maxey and Mary B. Anderson; 56 ac.; joining James Slaton, Beazley's old lines and George Chambers; March 23, 1826.

John M. Walker; 5½ ac.; joining lines of John M. Walker and William Moore; April 6, 1826.

**Page 201**

John Couch and William Anderson; 170 ac.; some small branches of Rock Island Creek joining lines and land formerly Price Perkins and now owned by Doct John Chant, John Briants, and James Tapscotts; December 12, 1832.

Doer John W. Gantt; 15 ac.; joining lines of Harris formerly Jefferson's February 26, 1833.

Willis Piller; 150 ac.; by virtue of his land office Treasury Warrant for 150 acres No. 6947 and dated September 14, 1820 Issued to Nathl A. Crenshaw and assigned to said Willis Piller by said Crenshaw on both sides Rocky Ridge joining Turpin alias Hubbard formerly Henry Baird William Molloy decd, Childress', Coleman and Seaymor Holman. On the plat William Molloy is shown as Widow Molloy).

**Page 202**

Edward W. Sims by virtue of his land office treasury warrant for 50 acres of land No. 12345 dated 24 March 1835; 4 acres on south side Slate River adjoining south bank of the Virginia Mill land John S. and George W. Nicholas; November 16, 1835.

James Harris; 114 ac.; by the land office treasury warrant for 150 acres No. 12405 dated October 1, 1835; adjoining Thomas Agee, Reed Brooks, William H. Allen, decd, William Snoddy, estate of Thomas Agee decd; May 11, 1836.

John L. Slaton; 25 ac.; adjacent Tapscott, Hamner, Joseph Cunningham, and Davis; July 20, 1836.

**Page 203**

John Hocker; March 9, 1843; 20 ac.; by virtue of a certificate from the land treasury warrant No. 3150 dated May 8, 1801 for 150 acres issued to Philip Hodnett and assistant to John C. Patteson and by survey made January 14, 1837; 130 acres for Patteson, leaves 20 acres for said warrant. Joining Long, Walker and Sergeant; 1845 -- additional notes indicate survey.

Thomas Hughes; November 28, 1943; treasury warrant for 50 acres No. 14076; May 26, 1838 issued to Stephen Guerrant assigned by him to Hughes 16½ ac.;

south side Slate River joining Berford and Sims, William Lightfoot.

Thomas D. Patteson and John E. Patteson; May 14, 1844; 7½ ac.; on treasury warrant for 25 acres, No. 15329, dated 11 April 1844; joining Cabbels old road, Col. John Harris, David Poor, the rest is illegible. Abraham Poor listed as a neighbor.

Page 204

William H. Tapscott; 150 ac.; December 12, 1844; joining Hamner, Thomas Cobbs, Tapscotts own lines.

Robert Moore; 15 ac.; assignee illegible; November 4, 1845; treasury warrant No. 7758 dated 1824; adjoining his mountain home tract and formerly Col. John Cabell's.

William T. Davidson; October 15, 1846; by treasury warrant No. 15437 dated December 3, 1844; 150 ac.; February 7, 1846; 234 acres in survey joining Clopton, Pickshim Road, Gilliam's, Webb, Dr. D. R. Patteson.

Page 205

William D. Jones and James Anderson (crossed out); Jones warrant for 500 acres No. 10249 dated 6 March 1829, 11 acres, east side of the road leading from Buckingham Court House to the new store joining James Anderson, Hooper's legatees and Judith Walker; June 22, 1836.

Capt Thomas Miller; treasury warrant for 30 acres No. 12403 dated September 24, 1835; 21 acres joining Weeks, Thomas Miller, Samuel Glover; October 4, 1835.

John C. Patteson; treasury warrant for 150 acres No. 3150 dated May 8, 1801; 130 acres joining Whetstone Branch, Charles Rice, Langhorne, Warner Williams now Dr. Anderson, estate of Morriss M. Langhorne, Stone Branch; above warrant issued to Phil Hodnett as per above data.

Page 206

Moses Flood, 12 ac.; May 10, 18??; bounded by his own land; (rejected).

Survey owner's name cut off; May 10, 1837; joining Richard Gilliam, William Sanders.

John Couch and William Anderson; May 13, 18??; joining Dr. John W. Gantt.

William Slaton; 250 ac.; by virtue of his two land warrants, one for 75 acres No. 10468 dated September 8, 1830 and other for 150 acres No. 11008 dated September 8, 1830; 250 acres joining Charles A. Scott, Warren Road, Benjamine Slaton, John Neighbour and Beasley on Rock Island Creek.

Page 207

William -----; October 16, 1846; treasury warrant 150 acres; February 7, 1846; 16 acres joining Harrison and Webb and Richard Lee.

Survey in division; November 11, 1848; 542½ ac.; belonging to estate of Reuben Seay, decd for legatees by their consent; O. S. Ayres 109 ac.; John Ayres 105 ac.; 113 3/4 ac. Benjamin Seay; Abner Seay 69½ ac; Nancy and John Seay 145 ac.; later parcel contains dwelling house on Bells Road adjoining Thornton J. White, Adcock and Benjamin Seay.

John C. Turner; March 1849; 343 ac.; belonging to estate of Fleming Turner decd for John C. Turner; W. S. Turner receives 61 acres of the total.

Page 208

Survey of 108 acres taken from estate of John Chambers; March 1849 for Willis (?) Chambers joining estate of Fleming Turner decd.

Survey of 25 acres taken from the estate of John Agee decd for James Agee by the request of Thomas Agee; September 30, 1848; signed N. A. Holman.

Survey of 26 3/4 acres made for William Shepherd to James Huddleston; October 20, 1858. Signed Samuel C. Wilkinson, surveyor Buckingham County; shows a new road.

Page 209

Survey of 3,188 acres divided among the legatees of Charles Irving decd by order of the court; September 30, 1803. On Fluvannah River joining David Patteson, Tandy Rice, Thomas Anderson dec.; Legatees: Robt Irving, lot 1 300 ac.; Charles Irving, lot 2 323 ac.; Mildred Irving lot 3, 323 ac.; Patrick Rose, lot 4, 323 acres; Paulus P. Irving, lot 5 342 ac.; Mrs. Roses dowery, 1577 acres (shows a dwelling house and a mill, plus 22 acres of vacant land); also shows the location in all parcels of high and low lands.

Pages 210, 211 and 212

This is a very large survey covering entire pages with the edges in poor condition. Land on Megginson's Road; joining John Spears, David Kyle, new lines, George Birks; shows Findley Creek; adjoining Megginson; On page 211: names on survey are John Radford, William Goff, William Cabell; on Shirley's Creek, Colo. John Cabell, Rakes, Mallory John, Col. Smith, James Webb; on Ireland Creek; shows the river; shows Bishops Creek; On page 212 these names appear: William(?) Spencer, 200 acres; John Hopkins, David Patteson, Spencer, on Sycamore Creek; shows the river; David Pryor; shows a dwelling house; shows Warminster Road; shows Joseph Cabells Road; Note: scraps of other surveys are also photographed alongside this survey, apparently dating from the 1770s. The surveys on these pages are jumbled but appear to be from one large map.

Page 213

This is a list of lands claimed prior to the survey and also of lands sold since the survey was made (vizt)(of prior claims). It probably relates to the plats on pages 210, 211 and 212.
Thomas Moseley's -- 400
Joshua Taylor --351
Connelley Mullins -- 260
James Boyd -- 156
Thomas Smith -- 325
Thomas Wright -- 232
William Briant -- 126
Nicholas Conner -- 504 (?)
Francis Amos -- 518
William Amos -- 231
  total -- 3121
Sold since survey was made:
to William Spencer -- 200
to Farrel McFadian -- 125
to Cary Harrison -- 600
to Thomas Livesay -- 1000
to Brett Randolph -- 6000
  grand total -- 11, 046 acres
Remains to David Bell:
  on Pickshin Road -- 549 ac
  within F. McFadian's plat --125
New total: 11,720 acres
Teste: Henry Bell, surveyor for Buckingham County.

(Presumably this is a plat of the lands of Henry Bell)

Page 214

Plat of 620 acres belonging also to the heirs of John Patteson decd to wit: Samuel Patteson, John Patteson, on waters of Appomattox River, joining Moses Swiney, James Patteson, James Wilkinson, estate of John Christian decd, and Thomas Logwood; divided as follows: equally divided land gives **Samuel Patteson lot 1 of 310 acres at upper end** of said tract and gives John Patteson 310 acres as lot 2 at lower end; dated 1807 by John Harris, assistant surveyor; Note: plat on this page is a continuation of plat on page 213 and does not relate to division of John Patteson's estate; the actual survey for Patteson's estate is on page 215.

Page 215 and Page 216

These two pages cover one plat with no date; Plat and dividend of 840 acres on both sides Elk Creek adjoining Phillip Duval, Widow Moses, Maj. Samuel Duval, Peter Moses, William Bradley, James Doss, Edward Doss, Nathan Neighbours, John Henderson, Capt. Charles Phelps; belonging to the heirs of John Patteson, dec'd (viz.) Capt Charles Phelps and Samuel P. Christian and the dower of Mrs. Ann Patteson, taken out of each of their lots. Shows dividing line; shows lot 1, 408 acres to Phelps with a dwelling house; lot 2 to Samuel P. Christian, 432 acres with dwelling house; shows lands reserved for the dower 71 acres, and 229 acres. Near Stillhouse Branch on Bent Creek Road; Note: This survey is very difficult to read.

Plat for George Carson; 490 ac.; joining Perkins, Joseph Watkins and Gresham Lee; no date.

## Page 217

Letter dated September 29, 1800 regarding the high court of chancery case dated March 1, 1799 involving James Cooper and Joseph Bondurant plaintiff and John Webb, defendant; signed John Patteson, surveyor; witnesses: William Taney (?), James Cooper, James Webb, and --- Davis.

Fragment of a survey containing these names: William Bradley, Thomas Thornhill, Mrs. Freeland, on Fluvanna River showing Wreck Island; no date.

## Page 218

Scraps of surveys containing these names:
William Briant -- 126 acres
Nicholas Conner -- 504 acres
----- Amos -- 518 acres
joining Francis Amos; Note: these apparently are fragments which attach to the survey on page 213 by Henry Bell.

Another survey for George Carson and George Billup for 140 acres, May 4, 1814; by virtue of their treasury warrant of 356½ acres No. 2195; March 8, 1814 joining Gresham Lee, George Carson, Capt. George Perkins, Joseph Watkins.

Scrap of a plat containing 14,720 acres of land surveyed for Colonel Joseph Cabell was this day compared and examined by me this 25th day of March 1794, teste, Henry Bell, surveyor, Buckingham County.

## Page 219

duplicate of page 218

INDEX

There are two parts to this index: a Personal Name Index and a Place Name Index. Page numbers are those of the ORIGINAL manuscript pages not the numbered pages of this book. Please check all possible spellings for a surname. Predominant spellings receive precedence in this index when the variant spellings are only slightly different. Check the Place Name section for surnames which are part of the name of a creek, road, etc.

Abotts
  Benjamin 126
Abraham
  Jacob L. 174
Adams
  John 176
Adcock
  ---- 207
  Anderson 16, 28, 98
  Carter 173
  George 98
  Henry 43
  Joseph 125
Agee
  ---- 109
  Hercules 115
  Jacob 103, 108, 109, 163
  James/Jas. 118, 158, 159, 187, 208
  John/Jno. 118, 208
  Joseph 185
  Mathew 4
  Noah 171, 185
  Thomas 202, 208
Akers
  William 12
Allen
  ---- 79, 171, 173, 185
  Elizabeth 163
  George 103, 146, 166, 171, 173, 175, 186
  George H. 62, 144, 163
  George Hunt 103
  John 63, 163, 166
  Mary 108 109
  Mr. 79, 155
  Philip 62, 163, 166
  Samuel 64
  William 48, 62, 103, 109, 149, 155, 163, 164, 165
  William (Capt.) 8, 103, 108, 164, 165
  William (Old Capt.) 166
  William H. 62, 103, 104, 108, 149, 202

Amg----
  William 6
Amonett
  ---- 63, 155
  Rueben/Reuben 171, 173, 185
  William 173
Amos
  ---- 123, 218
  Francis 22, 27, 28, 44, 124, 213, 218
  William 124, 213
Anderson
  ---- 189
  Charles 107
  George 147
  James 205
  John 150, 156
  Mary B. 150, 200
  Nathl 129, 130, 153
  Nathl (Capt.) 153
  Robert 98, 128, 182, 199
  Samuel 147, 190
  Thomas 41, 42, 47, 71, 77, 106, 129, 130, 151, 153, 209
  Thomas (Capt.) 94, 106, 130
  Thomas J. 165
  William 201, 206
Andrews
  William 194
Anglin
  William 4, 18, 43, 99
Arnold
  Benjamin 2
Arrington
  Adler 72
  Meves 39
  Samuel 32
Asher
  Thomas 48, 59
Austin
  Archelus 35, 46, 57, 69
  Nicholas 34
Ayres
  John 207
  Matthew 109

Ayres (cont'd)
  Nathan 71, 187
  O. S. 207
Baber/ Beaber
  ---- 111
  Thomas 153, 155
  William 7, 10, 43
Badberry
  William 146
Bagby
  Daniel 167, 176
  Daniel (Capt.) 153, 155, 169
  John 47, 116, 133, 134
Bailey
  Ben. 117
  Benjamin 178
  John 15
  Phill 117
  Robert S. 15
  Robert Spooner 6
Baird
  Henry 2, 201
Baker
  James 65
  Jerman 61, 186
Bakes
  Col. F. 5
Baky
  Jno. 183
Ballowe
  John 176
  Leonard 32, 33, 73, 144
  Thomas 14
  William C. 43
  William Cabell 42, 47
Banks
  Alexander 85, 105
Barksdale
  Hickerson 1, 20
Barnes
  John 96
Barton
  Nathaniel 123
Baskerville
  George 58
  John 61, 146, 154, 175, 186
Bates
  John 75
Battes
  Thomas 79
Beards
  ---- 92, 102

Beasley
  ---- 200, 206
  John 158
Beaver
  George 63
Beazeley/Beazely
  Charles 34, 71
  John 36, 46, 47, 75
Beckham/Beekham
  James 25, 35
Belcher
  James 186
Belekes
  James 61
Bell
  ---- 189
  David 45, 112, 112, 116, 119
    124, 131, 133, 124, 136, 213
  Henry 21, 61, 69, 82, 75, 97,
    98, 115, 116, 121, 122, 123,
    125, 128, 146, 218
  Judith (Mrs.) 61, 98
  Mrs. 98
Benning
  James 114
Berford
  ---- 203
Berks/Birks/Burks
  Elir(?) 13
  George 74, 210-212
  John 40, 61, 147, 157, 175, 186
  Joseph 112, 178
  Mrs. 130
  Sarah (Mrs.) 58
  Samuel 174, 181
Bernard
  John 95
  Jno. 53
  William B. 108
  William R. 103, 110
Berriman/Berryman
  Isaac 53, 63
  William I. 176
Bigbie
  William 161, 188
Billups
  ---- 91
  George 91, 123, 198, 218
Blackbourn/Blackburn
  Lambeth T. 16
  Lambeth Tye 19
  Thomas 37, 89. 110

Blakey
  Mrs. 182
  Thomas 21, 33
Blankenship
  Gad 105, 112
Blanks
  Robert 96
  Widow 170
Boatwright
  ---- 129, 133
Boaz
  Abednego 101, 118
  Meshack 193
  Thomas 21
Bolling
  Archibald 143
  Col. 2
  Lenaius/Laeneaus/Leneous/Lineus
    95, 105, 156, 194, 200
  Powhatan
    69, 75, 79, 100
  Robert 16, 75
  Robert (Colo) 75
Bondurant
  Benjamin 114
  Darbe/Darby 44, 94, 106, 114, 178, 181
  David 111, 114, 127
  John 18
  Joseph 217
  Pet. 4
  Peter 48
  R. 111
  Richard 105, 112
  Thomas 180, 113, 173
Booker
  George (Capt) 195
Booth
  ---- 147
  John 35, 83, 84, 87
Bostick
  John 36, 37
Bowcock
  John 21
Bowman
  ---- 161
Boyd
  James 26, 124, 213
Braber(Baber?)
  George 114
Bradley
  John 65

Bradley (cont'd)
  Joseph 66
  William 92, 215-216, 217
Branch
  Martha 109
  Matthew 109, 110, 122, 167
  Samuel (Capt) 199
Bransford
  ---- 163, 166
  Thomas 171, 185
Breckenridge
  John 73, 107
Briant/Bryant
  ----174
  Anthony 170
  Austin 169
  John 69, 94, 99, 121, 130, 143, 169, 201
  William 28, 121, 123, 124, 213, 218
Bristoe/Bristow
  James 61
  John/Jno. 197
Brooks
  Dudley 140
  Reed 202
  William 197
Brothers
  ---- 126
  John 38, 39, 125, 132, 154
  Thomas 142
Brown
  Benajah 187
  Cooper 67
  Isham 124
  John 23, 24, 124
  John J. 155, 187
  Jos. 81
  Joseph 81, 82, 85, 91, 92, 179, 195
  William 179, 195
Burnett
  ---- 92, 93, 102
  James 23, 24, 67, 142
Burton
  Douglass 176
  Elizabeth 176
  Isaiah 10
  Jacob 176
  Jane 176
  Micajah 176
  Nathl/Nathaniel 51, 52, 112, 176

Burton (cont'd)
  Patsy 176
  Robin 176
Cabell
  ---- 131, 133
  James (Col.) 17
  John 13, 54, 64, 68, 118, 121, 133, 161
  John (Colo.) 28, 64, 74, 116, 133, 183, 204, 210-212, 218
  John (Colo. Esq.) 74
  Joseph 67, 68, 70, 73, 74, 76, 77, 116, 210-212
  Jos. (Colo) 25, 57, 58
  Joseph (Colo) 33, 46, 49, 56, 60, 68, 71, 73, 75, 76, 78, 81, 87, 123
  Joseph (Esq.) 79
  Joseph (Senr.) 73
  N. 73
  Nicholas 70, 72
  William 210-212
  William (Doctor) 30
Call
  Charles 64
Carey/Cary
  A. (Honorable, Esq.) 28
  Archibald 100, 147
  Archd (Colo) 128
  Archd (Esq) 53
  Henry 98, 128, 147
  Robert 43, 99
Carr
  ---- 187
Carringdon/Carrington
  George (Colo) 20
  George 96
Carson
  Ezekiel 26
  George 91, 123, 189, 197, 198, 215-216, 218
Carter
  George 51, 95
  Joseph 97
  N. 158
  Thomas 94, 174
Cason
  Mr. 44
Cass
  Hugh 4
Cattrell/Cottrell
  Charles 43, 118
  Jacob 111
  Richard 154

Chalton (see also Shelton)
  Jacob 114
Chambers
  Edward 199
  George 2, 200
  John 31, 150, 173, 208
  John (Capt) 84
  Josias 140
  Josiah 42, 73, 79
  William 42
  Willis (?) 208
Chancellor
  Thomas 88, 90, 188
Chandler
  ---- 195
  George 151, 158
  Isaac 59, 60
  Jesse 139
Chastain
  Peter 109
  Rane/Reane/Rene 21, 109, 166, 171
Cheadle
  John 108
Chick/Cheek
  ---- 142
  William 80, 149, 157, 175, 186
Chenault
  Stephen 3, 10
Chernetter
  Issac 41
Childers
  John 37
Childress
  ---- 201
  Elizabeth 145
  Francis 10
  Francis Ware 63, 95, 100
  James 84
  John 3, 84, 90, 95, 129, 136, 160, 178
  Widow 145
Chiles
  Mr. 55
Christian
  ---- 20, 39, 65, 146
  George 112, 178
  James 17, 18, 19, 38, 99
  John 83, 162, 175, 186, 214
  Lewis 28
  Mr. 40
  Samuel P. 168, 182, 215-216
  Thomas 98, 173
  Turner 30

Clark/Clarke
---- 4
William 23, 24
Clay
---- 172
Clopton
  Reubin 86
  Robert 86
Coatsby
  George 29
Cobbs
  Elizth C. 166
  Richard 166
  Thomas (J.R.) 94
  Thomas 106, 130, 170, 174, 204
  Thos 130
Cock/Cocke
  David (P) 162
  John H. 96
Coffee
  Joshua 160
  Pleasant 160
  William 93, 102, 118, 160
Coleman
  ---- 201
  Grizzel 61
  James 55
  John 7, 8, 132
  Robert 131, 132, 141
  Saml 38, 78, 99, 132, 141
Colland/Calland
  Joseph 4, 101
Collins
  Joseph May = Collins 125
Conner/Conners
  Arthur 101, 118
  John 71
  Nicholas 9, 22, 25, 27, 28, 46, 55, 71, 121, 123, 124, 213, 218
Cooper
  James 217
Corder/Corker
  Robert M. 150, 158, 179
Coseley
  W. 28
Cotheel
  Charles 48
Cotteral/Cottrell see also Cattrell
  Benjamin 49
  Charles 94
  Jacob 85

Couch/Counch/Crouch
  ----85, 94
  James 42, 48, 71, 94, 174, 178
  James Bartlett 127
  Jas. 130
  Jesse 181
  John 21, 77, 201, 206
  John (Capt) 37, 46, 165, 178, 181
  Mrs. 165
Coupland
  ---- 189
Cox
  John 7, 8, 44
  Mary Kincaid 122
  Matt 196
Craig/Craigg
  Mr. 105
  Robert 113, 120, 121, 127, 128, 180
Creasey
  William 125, 126
Crenshaw
  Nathl A. 201
Crews
  James 120
Cunningham
  Jas. 169
  Jos. 163
  Joseph 69, 94, 115, 144, 202
Curd
  Edward 142, 180
  John 142
  Jos (Mr.) 51
  William 1, 142
Curree
  Reuben 80
Damron
  Michael 42, 47
Damson
  George 21
David
  Peter 63
Davidson
  David 44
  Jno 94
  William T. 204
Davis
  ---- 217
  Bartlett 53
  Peter 46
  Thomas 182

Day
  John 129
  Peter 24, 41
Dibrell/Dibraill/Dubral
  ---- 33
  Anthony 25, 32, 33, 36, 174, 182
Dilliard
  James 65
Dillon
  William 199
Diuguid
  ---- 65
  George 78, 80, 88
  George E. 161
  Lydia 178
  William 4, 11, 22, 24, 65, 66, 72, 87
Dixon
  John 84
Dobbins
  James Hundly 48
  Mr. 59
Dolan/Dolling/Doland
  Brian 4
  Briant 9, 27, 28, 121
  James 64
  John 64, 69, 113, 136, 170, 190
  Lee 71
  Mr. 34
Doram/Dorum
  James 46, 124
  John 124
Doss
  ----- 65
  Edward 215-216
  James 215-216
  Jesse 126
  Mark 8, 10
  Mr. 77
  Thomas 24, 25, 41
Drake
  Joel 52, 59
Duncan
  Jacob 109
  John 44
Dunkards
  Dancey 126
Dupeay
  Peter 156
Duval/Duvall
  Phil. 83, 162
  Phillip 215-216
  Samuel (Maj) 215-216

Easley
  ---- 20
  Robert 104, 108
East
  Thomas 151
Eldridge
  George 187
  Rolfe 97, 107, 158, 159, 198
  Rolfe (Sr.) 158, 159
  Rolfe (Jr.) 159, 167
Elgin/Elgun
  John 80, 87, 125, 126, 132
Elkins
  ---- 66
Ellyson
  T. 175
  Thomas 39, 40, 61, 127, 146, 154, 157, 186
Epperson
  ---- 19, 21, 125
  John 50, 95, 105, 144
  Joseph 3, 10, 12
  Littlebury 2
  Nath 21
  Richard 12
Evans/Eavins
  ---- 142
  Eliza. 97
  Elizabeth 99
  Joseph 14, 97, 159
  Williams 181
Evit
  Nehemiah 60
Falwell
  ---- 148, 179, 195
  John 94, 169
Faubush (?)
  Alexander 148, 179
Fearn
  John 96
Fergeson/Ferguson
  Dougald 129, 142
  Edward 26
  Joel 93, 125
  John 44, 75, 122, 125, 127, 131, 136, 142
  Robert 93, 102
  William 26
Fields
  John 25
Finch
  Nathl. 16

Fishers
  ---- 187
Flood
  ---- 118
  Henry 52, 90, 101
  John 62, 64, 103
  Major 161
  Moses 82, 113, 150, 206
  Noah 148
  William 187
Flower/Flowers
  Andrew 27, 39, 40, 87, 126, 127, 144
  David 101
  James 173
  John 9, 126, 148
  Ralph 22, 27, 55
  Roling 71
  William 21, 87, 119, 126
Forbes
  Alex. 195
  John 190
Ford
  ---- 166, 173
  Boaz 159, 173
  James 48
  John 66
  Stephen 108, 109
  William 37
Fore/Foree
  ---- 114
  Peter 43
  William 120, 122
Fowle
  ---- 179
Fox
  James 23
Freeland
  ---- 76, 80, 142
  James 15, 148
  Jas. 157
  Mace 63, 80, 142, 146, 157, 175
  Mase 50
  Mrs. 97, 217
  Robert 39, 40
  Widow 79
Fry
  Col. 2, 3
  John (Colo.) 21
  Joshua 2, 63
  Mr. 51
  William 177
  William A. 98

Fuqua
  Stephen 129
  William 52, 101
Gadbury/Galberry
  William 59, 80
Gallahorn/Gallohorn
  ---- 148, 151
  Charles 92, 93
Galloway
  Terry, 103, 104, 163
Gannaway/Gannoway
  Gregory/Grigory 120
  John 7, 181
Garland
  Griffin 5, 138, 144
  Jeremiah 5
  Jesse 99
  William 3
Garnett
  Armistead 95, 103, 160
  Nathanield 160
Garrett/Garrott
  Alex 171
  Charles 52
  Isaac 52, 101
  Nathanial 19, 143, 177. 178
  Stephen 71
Garvin
  William 157
Gary
  John 174, 196
  Thomas 196
Gay
  William 189
Ghant
  John (Doct) 201, 206
Gibson/Gipson
  Edward 62
  John 122
  Joshua 94
  Miles 25, 174
  Thomas 101, 102, 118
  William 111, 122, 137, 177
Gill
  Josiah 92, 93
  William 172
Gilliam/Guilliam
  ----118, 204
  David 81, 85
  Epaphroditus 16, 88, 89, 110
  James 141, 148
  John 84, 90, 136

Gilliam (cont'd)
  Jno 82
  Mr. 84
  R. 82
  Richard 85, 86, 88, 89, 110, 113,
    117, 136, 138, 140, 141, 197,
    206
  Sherwood 150
  Widow 82, 94
  William 7, 10, 19, 24, 25, 35, 90
    91
Glover
  Benjamin 197
  David W. 193
  Edmond 197, 198
  George 197
  James 197
  John 4
  Judith 197
  Lucy 197
  Patsy 197
  Robert 44
  Samuel 4, 205
  Thomas 197
  William 197
Goatherd/Gothard
  John Byron 29, 50
  John B. 39, 132
Godsey
  Judith 82
Goff
  William 36, 56, 57, 71, 87,
    210-212
Goffey
  William 102
Goings/Goins/Gowing
  ---- 61
  William 29, 50,149
Gollyhorne
  Charles 59
Goode
  Joseph 44, 114
Goodsey/Godsey
  Judith 52, 107
  Thomas 19
Gordan
  ---- 38
  Ann 39
  Nortly 38, 39, 40, 154
Goss
  Benj. 18
Green
  ---- 150

Green (cont'd)
  Gran Berry or Green Berry 113, 118
  Mr. 82
Gregory/Grigory/Griggory
  Tho. 37
  Thomas 84, 89, 90
  William 1, 12, 95, 108, 122
Gresham
  John 98, 128, 147
Grey/Gray
  James 2, 12
Griffiths
  Zachariah 141
Grizzle/Grizzles
  Henry 97, 187
Guerrant
  Daniel 109, 170, 171, 196
  John 155, 176
  Peter 8, 62, 63, 108, 109, 153
    155, 158, 161, 163, 164, 169
    176
  Peter (Capt, Jr.) 152
  Peter (Capt, Old) 152
  Peter (Jr) 156
  Peter, (Senr) 164
  Stephen 155, 166, 185, 203
Gwin
  Ric'd 7
Hadgins
  Holloway 103
Hale
  Samuel 59
Hales
  Peter 120
Hall
  ---- 16, 148, 151
  Mr. 51
  Samuel 135, 151, 162
  Thomas 111
Hamilton
  Henry 144
Hamner
  ---- 202, 204
  Charles 193, 194
  Charles W. 193
Hancock
  Mr. 52
Handsford/Hansford
  ---- 176
  William 42, 96, 161
Hardiman
  John 26, 116, 119, 124, 136,
    154, 156
  Richard 154

Hardwick
  Benja. 141
  Thomas 62
Hargrove
  ---- 91
Harris/Harriss
  ---- 131, 201
  Benjm (Capt) 149
  Claiborn 191
  Frances 111
  Francis 137
  James 202
  John/Jno 109, 112, 117, 124, 130, 153, 157, 178, 214
  John (Colo) 29, 31, 64, 68, 203
  John (Jr) 161
  Jordan 133, 135
  Joseph 109
  Mr. 149
  Obadiah 172
Harrison
  ----75, 141, 207
  Benjm. 139
  Carey/Cary 75, 97, 108, 117, 119, 128, 148, 149, 158, 162, 174, 179, 213
  Randolph 167
Harry
  Mr. 53
Harvie/Harvey
  Ellyson 149
  Thomas 44
Hatcher
  Josiah 137, 146
Hays/Hay
  ---- 3
  John 5
  Eliza. 5
  John Booker 23
  Nicholas 26
Hazlewood
  Cliff 101
  John 101
Head
  Thomas 26, 28, 121
Henderson
  John 126, 194, 215-216
Hendrick
  Elijah H. 180
Hennesey
  ---- 183
Hensley
  William 19, 24, 45, 52

Hill
  ---- 130, 163
  James 46
  Robert 153
  Thomas 24
Hilton/Helton
  ----50, 76
  George 30, 79
Hite
  ---- 66
Hobson
  M. 142
Hocker
  John 203
Hodges
  Benj. 20
  Benjamin 56
Hodnell/Hodnett
  Phill 180, 203, 205
Hoggart/Haggatt
  Nath. 1, 12
Holeman/Holman
  Holman's legatees 154
  Mrs. 114
  N. A. 208
  Seaymor 201
  Tandy 63
Holland
  Mr. 55
  Rich'd 55
Hood
  Nathl 143
Hooper
  ---- 145, 205
  Benjamin 178
  Elizabeth 177
  George 2, 21
  George (Colo) 104
  George (Gent) 21
  John 52, 63, 95, 105, 107
  William 160, 177
Hopkins
  John 68, 73, 76, 210-212
Horseley/Horsley/Horsly
  ---- 63, 76, 80, 142
  John 50, 63, 80, 126
  John (Colo) 200
  Joseph 147
Hoss
  John 4
Howard
  ---- 79

Howard (cont'd)
  Ben 15
  Benjamin 21, 70
  Nancy 66
  Mr. 69, 94
  William 71
Howell/ Howl/ Howle
  Charles 116
  Elizah 105, 112
  James 63, 114
Hubbard
  Hubbard alias Turpin 201
  James 181
Huddleston/Huddlestone
  James 208
  Robert 43
  Simon 97
Hudnett
  James 103
Hudson
  Samuel 34, 46
  Simon 106, 130, 181
Hughes
  John 3, 5
  Littlebury 167
  Thomas 203
Hundley
  James 25, 59, 75, 83, 162
Hunter
  ---- 125
  John 4, 5, 12
  Thompson 5
Irving
  Charles 68, 70, 72, 129, 149, 209
  Mildred 149 209
  Paulus A. 149
  Paulus P. 209
  Robert 149, 201
Isbell
  John 126
Jackson
  Henry 144
James
  John 68, 69
Jamison
  Daniel 173
  John 173
  Nancy 173
  Widow 173
Jefferson
  ---- 201
  Col. 10
  Randolph 43, 99, 121, 128, 146

Jefferson (cont'd)
  Randolph (Captn) 120
  Thomas 3, 188
Jefferies
  Jessee 185
Jennings
  John 13
  Samuel 139
  Widow 139
John/Johns
  James 120
  Mallary 36
  Mallory 56, 74, 210-212
  Widow 110
  William 120, 177
Johnson
  ----- 52
  Richard 133
  William 3
Jones
  Charles 49, 78, 198
  Edward 147
  Flamstead 68, 69
  John 44, 154
  John (Senr) 81
  Jonas 127
  Josias 15, 32, 34, 35, 147
  M. 119
  Michael 86, 112, 117, 119, 194
  Robert 152, 153
  Samuel 198
  Thomas 27, 162
  William 64, 81, 155
  William (Captn) 77
  William D. 199, 205
  William (Jr) 95
Jordan
  James 15
  Mr. 47
  Samuel 103, 109, 149
  Samuel (Colo) 55
Kelley
  George 136
  William 9
Kenneday
  William 32, 33
Kennon
  ----- 76, 79
  Mr. 50, 61
  William 175, 186
Kid/Kidd
  ----66, 154
  William 96

Kincaid
  ---- 109, 198
  Mary 122
  Robert 109, 122, 198
King
  Walter 20, 53
Kyle/Kyles
  David 39, 40, 66, 67, 77, 78, 92,
    132, 145, 148, 157, 196, 210-212
  Robert 39, 66
Land
  John 160
Landers
  Mathew 15
Langhorne
  ---- 205
  Morriss M. 205
Lawhorne
  ---- 104
Layne
  Charles 10, 11, 77
Leak
  William 34
Lee
  Evan 26
  Gresham 86, 89, 93, 96, 102, 123,
    139, 189, 197, 198, 215-216, 218
  John 9
  Richard 102, 119, 207
  Thomas 16
LeSeuer
  Chastain 97
  Samuel 97
Levilliam
  Anthony 64
Lewis
  Edward 167
Lightfoot
  William 203
Lipscomb
  Anderson 185
  Hezekiah 185
Livesay/Livesey/Livsey
  ---- 157
  Thomas 123, 133, 213
Lloyd/Loyd
  ---- 138
  Benjamin 144
Logwood
  Thomas 182, 214
Long
  Peggy 78

Low
  Beverley 42
  Daniel 69
  David 15
  Widow 69
  William 20
Loyd
  Mr. 95
Lumkin
  Widow 142
Lwelling
  Charles 120
Lynch
  ---- 107
Lyle
  James 40, 41
McCormick/McCormack
  David 16, 56, 57, 85, 138
  David W. 20
  Hugh 28, 133, 134
  John 56, 57
  Rebecca 195
  Saml 134
  Samuel 121, 134, 150, 161
  Thomas 138, 148, 179
  Sherwood 82, 150
  William W. 20
McCoseley,
  John 100
McCraw
  ---- 97
  Francis 118
  William 96, 97, 118, 125
McDonald,
  Mr. 32
McDowell
  James 26, 60, 92
McFadden/McFaddian
  Farrell 124, 213
  William 143
McKenny/McKinney
  Josiah 82, 92
  William 194
McLane
  ---- 199
McLoyd
  Rhoda 145, 159
  Widow 112
McMannaway
  John 35
McNeill
  James 46, 55

73

Mackisham/Markenshain
  Nehemiah 18, 48
Maddox
  ---- 96
  Claybourn 108
Mallory
  William 100
Maloy
  David 2
Markham
  Bernard 95
Markhams
  Ber. 117
Marshall
  John 103
Martin
  Stephen 167
Mathews/Matthews
  James 22, 29
  Philip 102
  T. 18
  Thomas 17, 18, 22, 23, 29, 31, 87, 113, 123, 124, 186
  Thos. 38, 45
  William 176
Maurain
  Jno 190
Maxey/Maxy
  ---- 180
  Ben. 116
  Benjamin 131, 161
  Bennet 150, 200
  Charles 33, 35, 46, 57, 64, 67, 68, 73, 116, 135
  Claborne/Claibourne 113, 170
  Edward 7, 51, 112, 173, 199
  Elisha 199
  Jacob 148, 190
  John 112
  Mary 94
  Nath'l 51
  Nathaniel 94, 129, 136
  Sampson 10
  William 26, 60, 82, 199
May
  ----128
  Charles 13, 112
  John (Sr) 11
  Joseph 125
  Joshua 11
  Peter 173
  Thomas 173, 198

Maynaird
  Nicholas 23
Mayo
  ---- 24, 72
Megginson
  ---- 210-212
  Joseph C. 74, 142, 148, 157
  William 10, 11, 17
Megruder
  ---- 160
Meredith
  James 9, 10, 15, 176
Merry
  Prettyman 196
Miller
  ---- 95, 99
  John 38, 40, 84, 98, 99, 104, 109, 112, 128, 141, 144, 145, 187
  John (Capt) 144
  Jno 22
  Thomas 191, 205
  Thomas (Capt) 205
Milton
  Isham 156
Mitchell
  Alexander 98
Molloy
  Widow 201
  William 201
Moon
  Little Berry 150
Moore/More
  ---- 183
  Benjamin/Benjm 55, 148, 149, 161
  Benjamin (Capt) 157
  Hugh 7
  Jno 183
  Robert 16, 43, 183, 204
  Thomas 183
  William 183, 193, 200
Morain
  John 140
Morris/Morriss
  ---- 149
  Benjamin 180
  Benjm 169
  Edward 84, 89
  John 57, 191
  Henry 31, 124
  Hudson 140, 190
  Nathl 169

Morris (cont'd)
  Nathaniel 177
  Tell (?)(Doct.) 192
  William 57, 84, 110, 117
  William (Jr) 82, 85, 90
  William (Sr) 88, 89
Morrow
  -- 142
  John 181
Mosby
  Little B. 32, 36, 87
  L. Barry 36
  Little Barry 49, 57, 78
Moseley/Mosley
  ----193
  Benjamin 71
  Benjm, (Major) 167
  C. (Capt) 117
  Charles 45, 112, 117, 119, 162
  Charles (Capt) 119, 124, 154
  Daniel 129, 196
  Francis 97
  John 27, 62, 105, 117
  John (Capt) 45, 52, 57, 116
  Robert 162
  Thomas 112, 124, 213
  William 116, 117
Moses
  Peter 66
  Widow 215-216
Moss
  Ann 127
  James 155
  Thomas 48
Mullins
  Connelley 124, 213
  Connerly 45
Murphey/Murphy
  ---- 105, 200
  Dennis 159
  Thomas Truman 4, 5, 95
Murray/Murrey/Murry
  Anthony 43, 85, 115
  Anthony (Capt) 111
  Mr. 120, 121
  Richard 10, 14
  William C. 146
  William O. 128
Neighbors/Neighbour
  Abraham 182
  John 206
  Nathan 77, 215-216

Nelson
  John 100
Neuman
  Thomas 5
Newcome
  Thomas 19
Newton
  William 97, 151
Nicholas
  ----- 21, 99, 104, 145
  George 96, 151, 153, 155, 158
    161, 167, 169, 170, 171
  George W. 202
  John 3, 10, 21, 55, 152, 192
  John S. 202
  Joshua 99, 104, 112, 143, 145
  Martha, Mrs. 200
  Mr. 156
  Mrs. 194
  Robert 151
  W. John 3
  Wilson 182
Nichols
  Wilson C. 140
North
  Anthony 178
  Gilbert 102
  Peter 157, 175, 186, 187
  Richard 87
  Richd 175
Northcut/Norcutt
  John 71, 75
  Nathan 4
  Widow 51
Nowlin/Nowling
  Abraham 188
  James 77
Nunnalle/Nunnally
  ---- 149
  Bernard 180
  Walter 97
Oakes
  Major 174
O'Brian
  Patrick 12, 21, 98, 105
Oglesby
  ---- 38, 65
  Richard 35
  Thomas 29, 30, 39
Page
  ---- 107, 185
  Carter 128

Page (cont'd)
  Edmund 107
  Edward L. 38, 142
  James 107
Palmore
  Joseph 44
Pankey
  John 64, 88, 124, 129, 131, 133,
    134, 136, 145
  Mr. 69
  Stephen 121
Parish/Parrish
  David 135, 150
  David (Capt) 54, 82
Parrow/Perrow
  ----103
  Charles 9, 55, 63, 103
Patteson/Pattison
  Ann 215-216
  Benjamin 31
  Charles 78, 85, 137
  Charles (Colo) 88
  Charles (Gent) 26
  Charles (O.R.) 17, 21
  D. R. (Dr.) 204
  David 23, 32, 33, 34, 70, 72, 73,
    79, 107, 165, 188, 209, 210-212
  David (A.B.) 23
  David (Major) 165, 181
  David R. (Doctr) 141
  Edward 45, 88, 92, 102, 119, 124,
    129, 131, 133, 187
  James 66, 71, 88, 90, 167, 188
  Jarrot 187
  Jas 161, 188
  John 16, 23, 74, 77, 81, 86, 89,
    93, 106, 121, 125, 126, 128,
    130, 137, 146, 150, 152, 157,
    161, 172, 174, 184, 188, 213,
    214, 215-216, 217
  John C. 210, 205
  John E. 203
  John (Jr) 23, 24, 33
  John (Senr) 67
  Leonard 42
  Nelson 112, 172
  Peter 88, 89, 90, 93, 125, 140,
    151, 161
  Samuel 193, 214
  Thomas 25, 33, 137, 145, 150
  Thomas D. 203
  William 23, 138, 140, 158, 190

Patterson
  William(Taylor) 29
Payne
  Charles 117
  Joseph 21, 96
Peak
  Richard 108, 139
  William 54
Peck
  John (Jr) 1
Pendleton
  ---- 39, 117
  Mac 79
  Mace 146, 175
  Widow 59
Penn
  Mrs. 126
Perkins
  ---- 215-216
  George (Capt) 189, 197, 218
  George 123, 151, 154, 175, 198
  Harden/Hardin 69, 71, 120, 146
  Harden (Capt) 43
  John 58, 68
  Price 99, 115, 120, 121, 130,
    153, 182, 201.
  William 78
  William (Capt) 35, 49, 57
Perrow
  Charles 151, 152, 158, 164
  Stephen 144
Phelps
  Charles (Capt) 215-216
  James 7, 8, 10, 11
  Thomas 23
  William 4, 5, 17, 20, 78, 88, 132
Philbottes/Philpott
  Edward 114
Philps
  Chas. (Capt) 168
Phipps
  Jones 149
Piller
  Willis 201
Pittman
  John 44, 81, 105, 107, 144
  Mr. 52
Pleasants
  Mr. 83
  Thomas E. 180
Poor/Pore
  Abraham 203

Poor (cont'd)
  David 203
  Elisha 40, 68, 78, 133, 135
Porter
  Rezin 162, 179, 195
Power
  Mr. 53
Price
  Thomas J. 171
  Thomas J. (Capt) 155
Pruitt
  Henry 14
Pryor
  David 47, 56, 58, 68, 77, 137, 146, 151, 210-212
  L. 151
Pucket/Puckett
  ---- 94
  Daniel 37, 41, 42, 46, 71
Purkins
  Harden 6
Puryear
  Reuben 137
Radford
  ----- 174
  John/Jno 57, 76, 78, 87, 116, 210-212
Rakes
  ----- 210-212
  Henry 64, 74
  William 36, 64, 67, 87
Randolph
  Brett 213
  Thomas 62
Ransone/Ransons
  Flamstead 55
  Robert 7
Rawlins
  Henry 98, 136
Ray
  ---- 156
  Moses 15
  Thos 130
Reach
  Nimrod 65
Reuben
  John 84
Revis
  Robert 129, 130
Rice
  Charles 205
  Davenport 69
  Edwin 69, 106, 130
  George 48, 59, 69, 75

Rice (cont'd)
  Rich. 114
  Tandy 209
Richardson
  Isham 113, 120
Ridgway
  John 2, 12
  Samuel 100, 177
Ripley
  Richard 78
Rives
  ---- 199, 200
  Robert 129, 153, 199
  Rives, McLane and Co. 199
Roberts
  ---- 16
Robertson
  Joseph 123
Rodgers
  David 40
  Jo. 126
  Robert 126, 127, 187
Roper
  Joseph 104, 143
Rory
  Peter 69
Rose
  Janne 149
  Mrs. 209
  Patrick 209
Ross
  David 167
Routen/Routon
  James 110
  John 37, 120, 122, 129, 136, 191
  Stephen 191, 196
Roy
  Peter 59, 75
Rudd
  James 16
Rye
  George 109
Sallee/Salley
  Isaac 5, 48, 52, 59, 114, 115, 154
  Jacob 111
Sanders
  ---- 166
  Daniel 97
  Edward 182
  James 177
  John 1, 97, 151, 178, 182
  John (Capt) 177

Sanders (cont'd)
  Robert 20
  Samuel 96
  Stephen 2, 180
  Thomas 34, 54
  William 206
Sanderson
  John 51
Saunders
  ---- 106, 142
  Daniel 63
  John (Capt) 106
  Samuel 110
  Samuel (Capt) 107, 113
Scott
  Charles A. 151, 206
  Joseph 55, 124
  Saymer 140, 178
  Scaymer 140
Scruggs
  Allen 144
  Finch 144
  John 53
  Micajah 197
  Vallantine 144
Sears
  John 139, 160
Seay
  Abner 104, 207
  Benjamin 207
  John 207
  Nancy 207
  Reuben 207
Sergeant
  ---- 203
Sharrons/ Sherrons
  ---- 103
  Arthr 166
Shelton
  Nelson 182
  Samuel (Capt) 165
Shepherd
  William 208
Sims
  Edward W. 202
Slaton
  Benjamine 206
  Charles 178
  James 181, 200
  James (Jr) 178, 181
  James (Sr) 181
  John L. 202

Slaton (cont'd)
  R. 178
  William 178, 206
Smith
  ---- 155, 190
  Abra 9
  Alexander 15, 24, 41, 87, 126, 127
  Col. 210-212
  Elizabeth 32
  Ellexer(?) 36
  Isaac 65
  James 32, 35, 57, 78
  John Terry 36
  Jeffrey 86
  Jeffrey Hardiman 116
  Jesse 127, 147
  Nicholas Vance Taverns alias Smith 117
  Obediah 83
  Patrick 52
  Robert 46, 55, 85, 89, 135, 139, 140, 150, 153
  Samuel 143, 179, 195
  Shadrach/Shadrah 88, 112, 178
  Thomas 26, 62, 102, 123, 124, 213
  Uriah 85
  William 127
  William (Colo) 74
Snead
  Henry R. 126
Snoddy/Snody
  James 173
  John 2
  Mr. 53
  William 202
Southern
  James 24.
Spears
  ---- 148
  James 79
  John 210-212
Spencer
  ---- 210-212
  Francis 124
  Mace 194
  Moses 162
  Samuel 72, 127
  William 46, 55, 116, 148, 156, 213
  William (?) 210-212
Stanley
  Thomas 65

Staples
  ---- 147
  Charles 183
  Issac 29, 30, 84
  J. (Capt) 181
  Jno (Capt) 165
  John 178
  Jno 183
  Samuel 90, 92, 102
  Thomas 50, 65, 75, 84, 87
  William 143
Statham(?)
  Charles 183
Staton
  Charles 46
  Chls 165
  Elijah 70
  Isham 70
  James 47, 70, 77, 106, 130, 150
    156
  John 47
  Reuben 70
  William 60, 70, 71, 75
Steger
  Sam 163
  William 163
Stephens/Stevens
  John 29, 30, 68, 77, 78, 82,
    134, 135
  Thomas 17, 29, 30, 31, 39, 40,
    75, 77
  William 75, 187
Still
  Thomas 24, 30, 31, 45
  Thos 72
  William 22, 30, 31
Stinson
  Alex. 1
  Cary 181
  David 181
Strange
  Jesse 40, 50, 59
  John B. 40
Street
  Dudley 137
Strong
  ---- 189
Suddarth
  John 71
Swiney
  Moses 89, 95, 214

Taliaferro
  ---- 142
Talley
  ---- 173
  Zacharia 53
Tabscott/Tapscott
  ---- 69, 127, 169, 202
  George 48, 178, 181
  James 201
  Mrs. 94,.106, 111, 181
  Widow 115, 130
  William H. 204
Taney (?)
  William 217
Tavern/Taverns (surname?)
  Nicholas Vanse 116, 118
Taylor
  ---- 19, 29, 75, 141
  Daniel 53
  Jarrat E. 127
  Joshua 27, 45, 124, 213
  Richard 17, 18, 22, 27, 30, 33,
    45, 65, 69, 75, 86, 102, 119
  Samuel 114
Terry
  James 174
  John 33, 36
Thomas
  G. 4
  Jesse 37
  John 41, 42
  Joseph 34
  Thomas 173
Thompson
  ---- 107
  Robert 97
Thornhill
  ---- 141
  Absolum 132, 134, 135, 141, 149
  Jessee 76
  Thomas/Thos. 5, 6, 9, 30, 50,
    92, 217
  Thomas T. 196
  William 22, 67, 77, 78, 132, 196
Tindal/Tindall
  Benjamin 152, 153
  Thomas 165, 188
Trent
  Alexander 198
  Thomas 90, 93, 101, 102, 118, 160
Tuggle/Tuggles
  John 127, 144

Turner
  Fleming 207, 208
  John 150
  John C 207
  Nicholas 157
  W. S. 207
Turpin
  ----alias Hubbard 201
  Colo. 11
  Thomas 48
  Thos. 18
Tye
  Allen 19, 45
Tyrie
  David 23
Vassar
  Andrew 87
Vest
  John 3, 10
  Jno. 99
Wade
  ---- 113
Wagstaff/Waggstaff
  ---- 31
  Francis 5, 18
Walke
  David 37
  Thomas 122
Walker
  ---- 91, 94, 203
  David 21, 54
  Henry 90, 91
  James 82, 84, 85, 89, 90, 91,
    108, 129, 136, 138
  James (Senr) 115
  John 54, 90, 91, 136, 175, 186
  John (M) 167, 183, 193, 200
  Jno 183, 190
  Judith 205
  Mrs. 193
  William 44
Walling
  Joseph 161
Walthall
  ---- 97
  Francis 97, 169
Walton
  ---- 155
  Edward 107
  Thomas 178
Ware
  Peter H. 147

Warner
  David 177
  Iverson 181
Warren
  William 20
Warriner
  David 138
Watkins
  J. 88
  Joel 86, 101, 108, 115, 125, 139
  Joel (Colo) 139
  John 156
  Joseph 123, 135, 139, 189, 197,
    215-216, 218
  Samuel 96, 115, 139,
  Silas 54
  Silas (Capt) 54, 101
  Spencer 178
Watson
  William 146, 154, 159
Webb
  ---- 204, 207
  George (Esq) 53
  James 210-212, 217
  John 89, 93, 119, 138, 141, 148,
    217
  Theodorick 21
  William (Jr) 90, 93
Weeklin
  William 3, 10
Weeks
  ---- 205
Welch
  James 56, 97, 107
Wells
  James 124
West
  Claiborne 177
  John 116, 137, 191
  Richard 150
  Rolin 156
Wheeler
  ---- 189
  Charles 28
White
  ---- 200
  Andrew 199
  Henry 103, 109
  Thornton J. 207
Whitebread
  Shachevel 5
  Shac 12

Whitney
  ---- 19
  Jeremiah 8, 38, 39
  Jeremiah (Gent) 17, 18, 19, 20,
    29, 58
  Mr. 61
  W. C. 17
Wilbourn
  William W. 196
Wilcox
  Susannah 189
Wilkinson/Wilkerson
  James 214
  Lewis 181
  Samuel C. 208
  W. 20, 53
Williams
  Nathaniel 144
  Rich'd 26
  Solomon 175, 186
  Warner 150, 151, 162, 194, 205
Wills
  Willis 126, 129, 140
Wilson
  ----- 109
  Colo. 174
  C. Wisdow(?) 189
  George 14
  James 105, 110, 138, 144, 189
  Matthew 109, 122, 192
Winfrey
  ---- 163
  Israel 59
  James W. 194
  John 106
  Ruben 42
  Samuel 75
Wingfield
  Thomas 44
Winiford
  Mrs. 180
Winston
  Edmund 122, 172
Witt
  Benjamin 25
  Charles 24
Woldridge/ Woolridge
  Henry 50, 145
  Joseph 138, 148
  Joseph (Capt) 195
  Thomas 51, 95, 97, 125

Womack
  Masanello 55
Wood
  Edmund 1, 13
  T. 97
  Thomas 36, 62, 125
  Thomas Ray 106
Woodall
  ---- 172
  John 2
Woodroff/Woodroof
  Harden 141
  Hardin 187
Woodson
  ---- 135
  Daniel 108
  Davenport 135
  Jacob 108, 115
  Jacob (Capt) 55
  John 139, 160, 176
Word
  Thomas 122
Worley
  John 40, 41
Wright
  Gabriel 172
  George 12
  James 132, 157
  John 1, 27, 28, 39, 80, 99,
    132, 149, 157, 170
  Robert 24
  Thomas 28, 29, 40, 50, 113, 123,
    124, 213
  Widow 172
  William 141
Yancey
  Charles 141
  Charles (Major) 138, 198
Zachery
  Bartholemew 26

PLACE NAME INDEX

Branches, Creeks, Rivers, etc.

Appomattox River
 1, 7, 12, 13, 23, 36, 36, 37, 44,
 89, 90, 93, 101, 102, 108, 115,
 118, 120, 122, 125, 135, 151, 160,
 197, 214
Arthur's Creek
 42, 107
Ballowe's Creek
 47, 149
Bear Branch
 38
Bear Creek
 38, 129
Bear Garden Creek
 155
Beaver Pond Creek
 22, 29, 31, 45, 75, 123, 124
Benning's Spring Branch
 114
Bent Creek
 4, 22, 30, 31, 39, 40, 44, 50,
 63, 78, 80, 141, 161, 168, 175,
 183, 215-216
Big Philipses Creek
 35, 57
Bishops Creek
 210-212
Bolling's Creek
 10, 16
Booring Branch
 167
Boring Branch
 38
Briants Creek
 5, 11, 122, 137, 198
Bridle Creek
 161
Broad Branch
 59, 186
Brook ---
 99
Buck Creek
 50
Buck and Doe Creek
 12, 19, 51, 63, 95, 97
Buckingham Branch
 98
Buffalo Creek
 109

Buffaloe Creek
 98
Cattail
 1
Ceaser's Spring Branch
 108
Childress' Creek
 3
Coleman's Run
 8
Crooked Creek
 109
Cycamore Island Creek (sic)
 23
David's Creek
 5, 6, 9, 14, 17, 18, 21, 22, 23,
 24, 29, 30, 39, 40, 80, 124, 134,
 142, 149, 157, 183, 187
Deep Bottom Creek
 166
Diuguid's Mill Creek
 11
Doe Creek
 2, 12
Double Trap Creek
 43
Dry Beaver Pond Creek
 123, 124
Dry Creek
 197
Elk Creek
 11, 215-216
Evat's Creek
 96
Findley Creek
 210-212
Fish Pond Creek
 16, 45, 59, 62, 92, 93, 102, 119,
 124, 135, 151, 158, 162, 179, 197
Fluvanna River (see also James River)
 6, 10, 13, 14, 15, 17, 18, 19, 25,
 29, 30, 40, 42, 61, 63, 72, 74, 79,
 80, 83, 92, 120, 146, 165, 170, 186,
 194, 209, 217
Freeland's Lick Branch
 10
Frisby's Creek
 27, 46

Fry's Branch
107
George's Creek (Big, Great, Little)
6, 10, 14, 43, 99
Glover's Creek
44, 122, 198
Great Buffalo Creek
62
Great Creek
7
Green's Creek
108, 109, 185
Halfway Branch
190
Hallman's Creek
42
Hardwick Branch
163, 166
Hatcher's Creek
21, 97, 98, 128, 147, 187, 190
Holladay/Holiday River
19, 20, 21, 82, 84, 85, 90, 91, 94, 138, 179, 195
Holloway River
54, 60
Holman's Creek 41, 42
Howl's Spring Branch
134
Hunt Creek
64
Hunt's Creek
8, 9, 62, 63, 103, 108, 153, 156, 158, 161, 163, 164, 192
Ireland Creek
36, 56, 65, 74, 210-212
Irons Creek
68, 78
James River (see also Fluvanna R.)
53, 70, 96, 170, 175, 176, 194
Jones Mill Creek
170, 190
Joseph's Creek
48
Lick Creek
32, 44
Little Buffalo Creek
61, 173
Little Fish Pond Creek
26
Little Philipses Creek
35, 57
Little Walton's Fork
58
Little Wreck Island Creek
39

Long and Hungry Creek
33
Long Branch
142
Long Branch Cattail
1
Main Ireland Creek
64
Meredith's Creek
57, 78
Middle Fork of Slate River
22
Middle River of Slate River
22, 26, 27, 28, 121
Mill Branch
164
Mill Quarter Branch
21
Mimm's Creek
9, 17
Mirus (?) Creek
127
Mountain Creek
100
Muddy Creek
75, 180
Negro Creek
74
Nothing Creek of Wreck Island Creek
25
Oak Branch
34
Old Doe Creek
64, 131
Old Woman's Creek
163
Phelp's Creek
53, 96
Phill's Branch
61, 88
Philip's Creek
15, 20, 35,
Phrieby's Creek
9
Polver's Creek
53
Pond Creek
156
Randolph's Creek
53, 176
Ransom's Creek 53, 176
Reyon's Creek
34
Ripley's Creek
49, 78, 137

Rock Island Creek
  6, 15, 34, 37, 41, 42, 46, 47, 48,
  60, 68, 69, 71, 94, 106, 114, 129,
  130, 153, 156, 178, 201, 206
Rocky Creek
  109, 144, 163
Sam's Creek
  19, 45
Sharps Creek
  43, 44, 111
Shirley's Creek
  210-212
Slate River
  4, 5, 7, 10, 12, 17, 19, 22, 25, 26,
  27, 28, 32, 33, 42, 44, 45, 55, 63,
  66, 71, 85, 89, 93, 100, 101, 109,
  112, 113, 114, 115, 116, 119, 121,
  122, 123, 138, 143, 144, 151, 155,
  161, 162, 163, 169, 192, 198, 202,
  203
Spencer's Creek
  32
Stephen's Creek
  6
Stillhouse Branch
  168, 215-216
Stone Branch 205
  205
Stonewall Creek
  143
Sycamore Creek
  210-212
Sycamore Island Creek
  67, 68, 72, 73, 76
Taylor's Creek
  33, 182
Thomas' Creek
  21
Thompsons Creek
  191
Tongue Quarter Creek
  3, 177
Troublesome Creek
  4, 5, 101
Turpin's Creek
  17, 97, 107, 114, 158, 173
Walker's Spring Branch
  91, 92
Walton's Fork
  25, 32, 33, 36, 56, 58, 174,
  182
Whetstone Branch
  205

Whispering Creek
  16, 185
White Oak Branch
  38, 39
Willis' Creek
  1, 2, 3, 12, 24, 96, 177
Willis' River
  16, 19, 20, 21, 43, 53, 57,
  62, 63, 88, 89, 97, 98, 99,
  100, 106, 107, 113, 118, 138,
  151, 180, 181, 182
Woodson Creek
  5
Wolf Creek
  26, 93, 102
Wreck Island Creek
  7, 8, 10, 17, 19, 20, 24, 25,
  29, 35, 39, 40, 41, 58, 61, 65,
  83, 84, 92, 126, 127, 146, 162,
  175, 186, 187, 188, 194, 217


OTHER PLACE NAMES

Allen's Quarter Road
  173
Amherst County
  63
Baird's Road
  21, 44, 138, 140, 148
Beard's Road
  20, 92, 102, 119, 195
Bell's Road
  207
Bell's Court house Road
  97
Belmont Tract
  61, 190
Bent Creek Road
  112, 168, 215-216
Bolling's Road
  43
Buckingham County
  12
Buckingham Courthouse
  146, 161, 180, 181, 183, 205
Buckingham Jail
  180
Buckingham Road
  21, 90, 93
Burnett's Road
  92, 93, 96, 102, 139

Cabell's Ferry Road
70, 72, 73, 87
Cabell's Old Road
203
Cabell's Road
17, 64, 56, 58, 67, 68, 210-212
Campbell County
143
Chesterfield County
74
Church Road
23, 163, 166
Coleman's Road
17, 41
Courthouse Road
5, 34, 69, 71, 111, 167
Cumberland County
19
Dr. Cabell's River Survey
30
Ferries
70, 72, 113, 114, 118, 120, 129
Furnace Land/Tract
103, 153, 155, 161, 164, 169, 170, 171
Glover's Road
5, 53, 137, 197
Gooding's Church
73, 75, 123
Gooding's Church Road
123
Godwin's Road
112
Goodwin's Church
114
Great Britain
20, 53
Great Road
16, 84
Guerrant's Gold Mine Tract
163
Hamilton's Ford
153, 161, 169, 158
High Court of Chancery, Richmond District
165, 175, 186, 192 (also Superior Court of Chancery, 198, 217)
Hooper's Road
122
Horn Quarter Road
98, 128
Howard's Church Road
60
Howard's Road
42, 43, 48, 59, 69, 70, 75, 178

Hunter's Road
5
Irving's ferry Road
129
James River Road
75
John's Courthouse Road
44, 107
Jones Road
44
Jordan's Road
85
Kennon's Mines
58, 61
Main Bedford Road
56
Main County Road
37
Marr's Road
43, 121
Matthew's Road
64
Megginson's Ferry Road
17, 118, 131, 210-212
Mills
165, 166, 170, 190, 198, 202
Moseley's Rolling Road
45, 117, 193
Mulberry Grove Tract
196
Murphy's Road
138, 150
"Musket and bayonet tract"
104
Naked Mountain
22, 88, 90
New Canton
140, 153, 161, 169, 170, 171, 184
New Canton Road
171
Old Tract Road
153, 158, 161, 169
Philip's Mine Survey
29, 30
Pickshin Road
9, 86, 119, 124, 154, 204, 213
Piney Mountain
30
Powhatan County Court
183
Prince Edward County
12, 160
Road from Buckingham Courthouse to Warren
146, 181

Road from Hamilton's ford to New Canton
  161, 169
Rocky Ridge
  2, 100, 201
Round Top
  3
Scottsville (also Albemarle Old Courthouse)
  113, 114, 120
Shelton's Mill
  165
Slate River Mountain
  10, 17, 45, 124
Thos. Matthew's Road 17, 124, 131
Tillotson Parish
  73, 75
Tract Road
  156
Virginia Mill land
  202
Walker's Road
  108
Warminster
  140
Warminster Road
  210-212
Warren (Albemarle County)
  71, 146, 181
Warren Road
  165, 178, 206
Willis' Mountain
  2, 3, 112, 145, 159
Willis' Swamp
  128
Winfree's "drillg house"
  75
Wreck Island
  186

www.ingramcontent.com/pod-product-compliance
Lightning Source LLC
Chambersburg PA
CBHW071227160426
43196CB00012B/2431